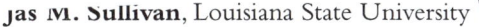

"*Historic Firsts in U.S. Electio*...
logical, and racial context su...
must-read for those interested

Jas M. Sullivan, Louisiana State University

"Truly pathbreaking candidates do not come along often. When they do, we need to understand how they campaign, mobilize support, and, if elected, do their work as representatives. This volume does that important work and should be read by scholars and politicians alike."

John M. Sides, Vanderbilt University

"This important and intersectional text moves beyond the *Historic Firsts* of Shirley Chisholm, Jesse Jackson, Hillary Clinton, and Barack Obama to offer superb analysis of gubernatorial, congressional, and mayoral historic firsts. The authors brilliantly demonstrate the limits as well as achievements of descriptive and substantive representation for historic candidacies across race, ethnicity, and gender. Simien's influential theory of symbolic empowerment undergirds this volume which helps to frame how scholars and practitioners should consider both multiracial and multiethnic constituencies in American behavioral studies. This is an essential text for anyone who seeks to better understand electoral outcomes via an intersectional lens."

Nadia E. Brown, Georgetown University

HISTORIC FIRSTS IN U.S. ELECTIONS

Historic Firsts in U.S. Elections: Trailblazing Candidates in Gubernatorial, Congressional, and Mayoral Campaigns examines barrier-breaking figures across various types of elective offices and constituent groups. The moment in which historic firsts enter the electoral arena, and the unique campaigns that ensue, are shown to be symbolically empowering. These change agents on the campaign trail become lighting rods for more liberal policies, and their candidacies are tied to questions of representation, electability, and performance. The distinctive combinations of race, ethnicity, and gender identities represented here translate into voter excitement to go to the polls and participate in other ways. Original chapters by respected scholars and practitioners consider how recent breakthrough elections are similar to yet different from past elections for gubernatorial, congressional, and mayoral offices. The shadow of Donald Trump's wildly unconventional U.S. presidency looms over this groundbreaking analysis, linking local to national level politics. For students of politics across the curriculum, this book expands the theoretical capacity of intersectionality research and links it to voter mobilization and electoral success

Evelyn M. Simien is Professor of Political Science and Director of the Indigeneity, Race, Ethnicity, and Politics (IREP) master's degree program at the University of Connecticut. She received her Ph.D. from Purdue University and specializes in intersectionality research, African-American politics, public opinion, and political behavior.

RACE, ETHNICITY, AND GENDER IN POLITICS AND POLICY

In collaboration with the Center for the Study of Race, Ethnicity, and Gender in the Social Sciences at Duke University

Series Editors: Kerry L. Haynie and Paula D. McClain

www.routledge.com/Race-Ethnicity-and-Gender-in-Politics-and-Policy/book-series/REGPP

This series is devoted to publishing studies that examine and explain the dramatic transformations in race, ethnicity, and gender politics over the past decade. We welcome work that highlights and analyzes the ways that race, ethnicity, and gender – and especially, their various intersections – interact to shape political institutions, individual attitudes and behaviors, social norms, and the policy-making process. Books in the series will include original scholarly research, core textbooks, supplementary topical books, and reference works.

Titles in the Series

Black Politics in Transition
Immigration, Suburbanization, and Gentrification
Edited by Candis Watts Smith and Christina M. Greer

Latinas and the Politics of Urban Spaces
Edited by Sharon A. Navarro and Lilliana Patricia Saldaña

Historic Firsts in U.S. Elections
Trailblazing Candidates in Gubernatorial, Congressional, and Mayoral Campaigns
Edited by Evelyn M. Simien

CV 07.07.2022 1400

HISTORIC FIRSTS IN U.S. ELECTIONS

Trailblazing Candidates in Gubernatorial, Congressional, and Mayoral Campaigns

Edited by Evelyn M. Simien

Routledge
Taylor & Francis Group

NEW YORK AND LONDON

First published 2022
by Routledge
605 Third Avenue, New York, NY 10158

and by Routledge
4 Park Square, Milton Park, Abingdon, Oxon, OX14 4RN

Routledge is an imprint of the Taylor & Francis Group, an informa business

Library of Congress Cataloging-in-Publication Data
Names: Simien, Evelyn M., 1974– editor.
Title: Historic firsts in U.S. elections : trailblazing candidates in gubernatorial, congressional, and mayoral campaigns / edited by Evelyn M. Simien.
Other titles: Historic firsts in United States elections
Description: New York, NY : Routledge, 2022. |
Series: Race, ethnicity, and gender in politics and policy |
Includes bibliographical references and index. |
Identifiers: LCCN 2021051845 (print) | LCCN 2021051846 (ebook) |
ISBN 9781032101569 (hardback) | ISBN 9781032101521 (paperback) |
ISBN 9781003213925 (ebook)
Subjects: LCSH: Elections–United States–History–21st century. |
African American politicians–History–21st century. | Women politicians–
United States–History–21st century. | Legislators–United States–
History–21st century. | Governors–United States–History–21st century. |
Mayors–United States–History–21st century.
Classification: LCC JK1965 .H564 2022 (print) |
LCC JK1965 (ebook) | DDC 324.973–dc23/eng/20211130
LC record available at https://lccn.loc.gov/2021051845
LC ebook record available at https://lccn.loc.gov/2021051846

ISBN: 978-1-032-10156-9 (hbk)
ISBN: 978-1-032-10152-1 (pbk)
ISBN: 978-1-003-21392-5 (ebk)

DOI: 10.4324/9781003213925

Typeset in Bembo
by Newgen Publishing UK

For my daughters, Skylar-Belle and Lillian-Reese

CONTENTS

FIGURES AND TABLES

Figures

Tables

CONTRIBUTORS

Sharon Wright Austin is Professor of Political Science at the University of Florida. Her research focuses on African-American political behavior, African-American mayoral elections, and rural African-American political activism. She is currently editing a book entitled *Political Black Girl Magic: The Elections and Governance of Black Female Mayors*.

Stefanie Chambers is Professor of Political Science and Department Chair at Trinity College in Hartford, CT. She is currently working on a documentary film, *Dreaming in Somali: New Americans in the Twin Cities*, based on her book *Somalis in the Twin Cities and Columbus: Immigrant Incorporation in New Destinations*.

Laurel Elder is a professor of Political Science at Hartwick College, where she teaches a wide range of courses within American Politics. Her third book, *The Partisan Gap: Why Democratic Women Get Elected But Republican Women Don't* is forthcoming with NYU press.

Lorrie Frasure is Vice Chair and Associate Professor of Political Science with a joint appointment in African-American Studies at the University of California-Los Angeles. Her current research is supported by the National Science Foundation, including the Collaborative Multiracial Post-Election Survey, a national, multi-racial/ethnic, multilingual study of socio-political behavior in the United States.

Chelsea N. Jones is a senior policy fellow at the Latino Politics and Policy Initiative and Ph.D. student in the Political Science Department at the University of California-Los Angeles. Her background is in social policy, having obtained a master's degree in Public Policy at Carnegie Mellon University.

Lauren E. Jones is the Executive Vice President at the Massachusetts Business Roundtable, focusing on policy and communications to develop strategies, initiatives, and programs consistent with the Roundtable's mission. Lauren holds a master's degree in Public Administration from Northeastern University and bachelor's degree in Political Science from Providence College.

Michael Minta is Professor of Political Science at the University of Minnesota. He received a Ph.D. in Political Science from the University of Michigan. His book *Oversight: Representing Black and Latino Interests in Congress* is a valuable guide for scholars, political leaders, and the legal community.

Crystal Robertson is a graduate research fellow at the Ralph J Bunche Center for African-American Studies. She is currently obtaining her Ph.D. in Political Science from the University of California, Los Angeles. Her research examines the role of social identities and their intersections in public opinion of social movements.

Evelyn M. Simien is Professor of Political Science and Director of the Indigeneity, Race, Ethnicity, and Politics (IREP) master's degree program at the University of Connecticut. She received her Ph.D. from Purdue University and specializes in intersectionality research, African-American politics, public opinion, and political behavior.

ACKNOWLEDGMENTS

The idea of this project started in fall semester 2019 when I first taught a variable topics course with the title, *Historic Firsts in U.S. Elections*, to a group of undergraduates at the University of Connecticut. This book would not have been completed without the research assistance of Aaron Hooker, who was also enrolled in the course. He easily mastered research skills that would put many graduate students to shame. I could not have asked for a more competent and reliable research assistant. Aden Abbatemarco, who picked up where Aaron left off, provided additional research assistance. Her attentiveness to detail and propensity to ask questions was extraordinary. Maman Cooper (a former undergraduate research assistant) also proofread select chapters before the manuscript went into production. She handled this task efficiently, providing thoughtful suggestions for improving the readability of the text. I am so very appreciative of their service. Additionally, I received small grants from the Africana Studies Institute, the College of Liberal Arts and Sciences, as well as the Office of the Vice President for Research at the University of Connecticut. I am especially thankful for this generous support, which was awarded at critical times prior to the coronavirus pandemic and the protests that followed George Floyd's death.

I am most grateful for the meaningful cross-pollination of ideas that helped to advance the theoretical framework at the heart of this book. I wish to thank all who attended our panel, *Historic Firsts in U.S. Elections*, at the 2021 annual meeting of the National Conference of Black Political Scientists (NCOBPS). It allowed contributors to meet virtually and discuss the implications of "historic first" candidates before a large virtual audience of interlocutors. One participant, however, deserves special recognition. Pei-te Lien asked thoughtful questions and made keen observations that influenced my own thinking about the concept of symbolic empowerment and historic first candidates—particularly, their ground game in diverse electoral contexts. Immediately following the panel, she sent me a follow-up email with an attached article. I found the work by Christian Collet (2008), as it appeared in *Perspectives on Politics*, on minority candidates and toggling most insightful. It informed both the introduction to this edited volume and my co-authored chapter with Lauren E. Jones on Ayanna Pressley. Again, I am most grateful for this recommended reading.

I wish to thank the Department of Political Science at Purdue University, who hosted me for a conversation on historic firsts and symbolic empowerment, as did several other universities over the last few years: Pennsylvania State University, Louisiana State University, University of Houston, Pitzer College, Brown University, Providence College, Trinity College, Wesleyan University, and Menlo College. My monograph, *Historic Firsts: How Symbolic Empowerment Changes U.S. Politics* (Oxford UP, 2015) was made available when possible, to their faculty and students in advance of these talks and increased sales. These audiences provided exceptional feedback that I used to advance this work, which I view as its sequel.

I am indebted to all the contributors who answered the call for papers, which overlapped with national conversations about race in the wake of George Floyd's death and culminated in calls for more diverse faculty, and other racial initiatives. I owe a special debt of gratitude to Laurel Elder and Stefanie Chambers who penned the response to our external reviews within days so the Press could issue a contract in advance of my delivery date for baby girl, Lillian-Reese. This book has been a few years in the making due to unique burdens created by COVID-19, disproportionate service in the aftermath of George Floyd's death, and a pregnancy that coincided with these unprecedented events. The protests that began in May 2020 in response to the death of George Floyd, Breonna Taylor, and others killed at the hands of police created an urgent need for our interpretative labor—that is, to help others within the university, discipline, and community writ large understand state sanctioned anti-Black violence. I, for example, was asked to create an online learning module within a few weeks for an Anti-Black Racism course that was offered by the University of Connecticut.

This kind of diversity-related service disproportionately fell upon the shoulders of women academics and faculty of color during a public health emergency of global concern. For women like myself with multiple roles—be they ethnic, gender, or familial—the coronavirus made it more difficult to find balance between different kinds of work (research, teaching, mentoring, and service) while at the same time stripping us of what supports—childcare—we had in place that better equipped us to strike a balance. The labor involved in meal preparation, helping children with remote learning, as well as caring for babies and young children exacts a physical toll. The growing demand for more web-based instruction and online communication made it increasingly difficult to set clear boundaries between our home and academic lives. It is reasonable to assume that since the pandemic faculty work hours have increased immeasurably to move classes to hybrid and online, accompanied by equally substantial changes in the allocation of roles and responsibilities at home, posing a catch-22 for women academics and faculty of color when research productivity counts most toward career advancement and new work-family crises have emerged due to the pandemic. Considering this, I am so very thankful that tenure and promotion is behind me.

An African-American woman at a major research institution with three small children under the age of 12, especially at the rank of full professor, I am truly an outlier in higher education generally and the political science discipline specifically. In the immediate aftermath of George Floyd's death and at the height of the coronavirus pandemic, I was asked to serve on the American Political Science Association's Presidential Task Force on Systemic Inequality in the Profession and charged with co-authoring a report with Sophia Jordán Wallace of the University of Washington for its working group on climate and context. Sophia and I worked extremely well together and co-authored a report on exclusion and disproportionate service burdens for women academics and faculty of color in the profession when this intellectual project was still a work in progress.

Carefully researching and synthesizing, as well as compiling data of considerable length to advance a strategic plan for equity and inclusion takes considerable time and is less highly regarded than a university press book, peer-reviewed journal article, or even a book chapter—that is, a valued publication comprised of original research that counts toward tenure and promotion and for which faculty are rewarded with merit pay. Being personally invested and viewing ourselves as change agents when asked to serve in this capacity constrains our ability to say "no" when we are mindful of the pervasive and persistent underrepresentation of women academics and faculty of color like ourselves in the profession. And so, we know first-hand that disproportionate service is not mitigated by our seniority. It was a pleasure to get to know and commiserate with Sophia over the challenges we face as women of color who desire to achieve a healthy work-life balance despite the service demands put upon us.

As someone whose partner is a sergeant major in the U.S. Army—the most senior rank of an enlisted soldier—I perform a larger share of the parenting and domestic tasks at home while he is stationed elsewhere. While attending a series of prenatal medical appointments and suffering from morning sickness throughout the course of a high-risk pregnancy, I experienced a great deal of stress and parental burnout as I faced intense pressures to meet work and family responsibilities during the pandemic. Still, I continued to mentor and advise students as well as serve on committees. I wish to thank Le'Roy for the days and weeks he has spent here with me to offset the burden. He drives from Kentucky to Connecticut monthly to offer me respite. We have known each other for 20 plus years, dating back to high school. He cooks meals, runs errands, does the grocery shopping, picks up and drops off kids, washes clothes, and lets me sleep in late. I am a night owl who often works into the wee hours of the night while the kids sleep, and there are many occasions when the baby nurses and falls asleep on a boppy pillow in my lap, dozes in a bouncer at my feet, or peers at me from a swing while I write.

I am also thankful for the consistent support I received from colleagues and friends during this time: Detris Adelabu, Sherman Benoit, Randolph Burnside, Stefanie Chambers, Jane Gordon, Lewis Gordon, Shareen Hertel, Lorraine Jones, Linda March, Tyson King-Meadows, Sharon LaTour, Shayla Nunnally, Jocelyn Remington, Elena Thomas, Linda Trautman, Jas Sullivan, Fiona Vernal, and Rhasaan Wilson. I so appreciate the home visits, gifts, text messages, phone calls, and emails.

I am grateful for the support provided by extended family members: Claudette Tousant and Tosha Tousant, who cared for my daughter Skylar-Belle when I went into labor and delivery for Lillian-Reese. My tween, Roman Marcellus, is also a godsend. This boy is an avid reader and obsesses about his grades. I am relieved by this fact. He assembles almost every toy, and device for his younger siblings. By the end of the day, he is routinely turning off every toy and device to conserve its battery life. Still a young adolescent, he often volunteers to get toddler girl ready in the mornings and keeps her entertained on the weekends, enduring her terrible twos with infinite poise and grace. To my chagrin, he introduces her to language I'd prefer she not hear like "What the heck!" and she later repeats incessantly. On Saturday mornings, he's often the first responder who takes her downstairs for "Mickey Mouse Clubhouse" and breakfast. Honestly, I don't know what I would do without him sometimes. Baby sister, who has us all ensnared with her coos, belts out the loudest cries. I affectionately call her "Lil-Reesey," big sis is "Sky-B," and Roman is simply "Ro-MAN." All three of these kids make life worth living to the fullest. Though I often feel like there's not enough hours in the day, I have no regrets despite the lack of sleep these days. I love motherhood.

I am grateful to my parents who made an investment in my academic future long ago. They always listened and supported my decisions, even when they feared being apart from me. Looking back, I think I took for granted the level of confidence they had in me. At a young age (in my early twenties), I uprooted and moved from the South to the Midwest for graduate school and assumed a tenure-track job in the Northeast. Unfortunately, this coronavirus pandemic and its variants along with the devastation of two hurricanes, massive flooding, and tornadoes hitting my hometown of Lake Charles, Louisiana have kept us apart far too long. I look forward to the day we can exchange hugs, and my mother can kiss these babies.

1

HISTORIC FIRSTS IN U.S. ELECTIONS

An Introduction

Evelyn M. Simien

Introduction

Do trailblazing candidates bring formerly politically inactive people into the electoral process? *Historic Firsts in U.S. Elections* examines barrier-breaking figures across various types of elective offices and constituent groups. At the heart of this book is a central, organizing concept—symbolic empowerment—that suggests historic firsts matter insofar as they mobilize new segments of the American electorate. The moment in which historic first candidates enter the electoral arena, and the campaigns that ensue, are described in terms of contextual effects that are symbolically empowering. The cumulative effect of their multiple identities and the historic nature of their campaigns stoke the desire to vote and participate in other ways, from attending a campaign rally and donating money to giving someone a ride to the polls, despite problems that arise in dealing with traditional opponents, from the injection of coded racial appeals or "dog whistles," to the distortion of their legislative records and altered images in commercial ads or political cartoons (López 2015; Phoenix 2020).

The presence of a historic first candidate who mirrors a marginalized group pictorially signals greater access to electoral opportunities and motivates political behavior from the kind of voters that political analysts would describe as being on the periphery of American politics looking in, if they are following campaigns at all. These races are hard fought, and the stakes are high especially when historic first candidates unite diverse electorates and establish multiracial coalitions in opposition to conservatives who seek to suppress votes and impose ballot restrictions. Loyalty, or a sense of belonging, to the group in question facilitates the process whereby a strong affective intragroup emotion like pride results in an ego-enhancing appraisal of the event and public figure associated with a socially

DOI: 10.4324/9781003213925-1

valued outcome—that being, in this case: the election of a historic first to public office (Lazarus 1991; Marcus, Newman, and MacKuen 2000; Parkinson, Fischer, and Manstead 2005; Finn and Glaser 2010; Sullivan 2014; Phoenix 2020; Burge 2020). They, who act as change agents on the campaign trail, emerge as lighting rods for more liberal and progressive public policies. As such, historic candidacies are inextricably tied to questions of representation, electability, and performance (Phillips 1995; Mansbridge 1999). That said, the shadow of Donald Trump's wildly unconventional 2016 election, his first term as an American president, the 2018 congressional midterm elections, and the 2020 American presidential election loom over this groundbreaking analysis.

In the months leading up to the 2018 congressional midterm and 2020 American presidential elections, journalists wrote in anticipation of several break-through contests. The 2018 midterm elections were markedly different from prior ones, with the Democrats gaining a total of 41 seats in the U.S. House of Representatives and assuming control of that chamber (Brown and Cassese 2020). A record number of historic first candidates had run for and won their parties' nomination for election to the U.S. House and Senate in 2018, and polls showed that several trailblazing candidates were running competitive guberna-torial campaigns at the same time. Many of whom aspired to become state and national leaders were diversifying American politics based on multiple axes of identity: age, race, ethnicity, sexual orientation, religion, indigeneity, etc. Twenty-four historic firsts were elected to serve as representatives in the U.S. House and Senate as well as state governors, twelve of whom were women of color (Epstein and Scott 2018; Hansen 2018; Levin and Wong 2018; Mak 2018). Still, others ran and won on the local level as city mayors. See Table 1.1 for a list of historic first candidates elected in 2018 to congressional and gubernatorial offices.

Why did 2018 produce such large gains for history-making firsts? A couple of factors combined to elect more diverse candidates to public office. These factors relate to the behavior of *both* the candidates *and* the voters. Record numbers of his-toric first candidates ran for the U.S. House and Senate in 2018, in part because of special circumstances that motivated them to seek election from Donald Trump's presidency and social movements #MeToo and #BlackLives Matter to the Supreme Court Justice Brett Kavanaugh's Senate Confirmation hearings (Brown and Cassese 2020; Castle et al. 2020). Arguably, the game-changing performances of historic first candidates necessitate an ongoing, research agenda on how candi-date identities [plural] mobilize new segments of the American electorate, in part due to higher voter turnout rates exhibited by women, racial and ethnic minor-ities, as well as younger age cohorts in recent elections.

Historic Firsts in U.S. Elections builds upon previous work by extending the sym-bolic empowerment framework to the Trump era, and by shifting the focus from the historic firsts of presidential campaigns—Shirley Chisholm and Jesse Jackson; Hillary Clinton and Barack Obama to recent history-making firsts of guber-natorial, congressional, and mayoral campaigns. In *Historic Firsts: How Symbolic*

TABLE 1.1 History-Making Firsts Elected in 2018 to U.S. Congressional and Gubernatorial Offices

Candidate	Political Party	History Making Firsts	Office	State
Cindy Axne	Democratic	Female	U.S. House	IA
Marsha Blackburn	Republican	Female	U.S. Senate	TN
Angie Craig	Democratic	Openly lesbian	U.S. House	MN
Sharice Davids	Democratic	Native American, openly lesbian	U.S. House	KS
Veronica Escobar	Democratic	Latina	U.S. House	TX
Abby Finkenauer	Democratic	Female	U.S. House	IA
Sylvia Garcia	Democratic	Latina	U.S. House	TX
Michele Lujan Grisham	Democratic	Latina	Governor	NM
Lou Leon Guerrero	Democratic	Female	Governor	GU
Deb Haaland	Democratic	Native American female	U.S. House	NM
Jahana Hayes	Democratic	Black female	U.S. House	CT
Cindy Hyde-Smith	Republican	Female	U.S. Senate	MS
Janet Mills	Democratic	Female	Governor	ME
Joseph Neguse	Democratic	Black male	U.S. House	CO
Kristi Noem	Republican	Female	Governor	SD
Alexandria Ocasio-Cortez	Democratic-Socialist	Youngest female	U.S. House	NY
Ilhan Omar	Democratic-Farmer-Labor	Somali American, Muslim female	U.S. House	MN
Chris Pappas	Democratic	Openly gay male	U.S. House	NH
Jared Polis	Democratic	Openly gay male	Governor	CO
Ayanna Pressley	Democratic	Black female	U.S. House	MA
Kim Reynolds	Republican	Female	Governor	IA
Kyrsten Sinema	Democratic	Openly bisexual female	U.S. Senate	AZ
Rashida Tlaib	Democratic-Socialist	Palestinian-American, Muslim female	U.S. House	MI
Lauren Underwood	Democratic	Black, female, millennial	U.S. House	IL

Note: N=24, compiled by the author based on data derived from Epstein and Scott 2018; Center for American Women and Politics (CAWP) 2018; Hansen 2018; Levin and Wong 2018; and Mak 2018.

Empowerment Changes U.S. Politics, I argued that the historic entry of the above presidential hopefuls changed the nature of American presidential elections (Simien 2015). I asked: Did their historic candidacies change levels of political engagement for various groups across race, ethnicity, and gender? While I examined the circumstances under which the changing face of American presidential politics boosts the premium that individuals assign to voting and other political behaviors, I also implored readers to consider the ways in which unconventional white candidates like Hillary Clinton use their gender and race to serve as a catalyst for white Americans in the voting booths. Whether such candidates achieve group solidarity on this basis remains a hugely important and timely question, given Trump's loss of his second term as president of the United States and the role in which Black voters played in determining the outcome of the 2020 American presidential election as they were the "margin of victory" in such battleground states as Michigan, Pennsylvania, and Georgia.

Significance of the Study

Now more than ever, research on the mobilization of American voters is vitally important for understanding the effect of historic firsts and their consequences for recent campaigns and elections as well as the future of democratic leadership in the United States (Simien 2015; Simien and Hampson 2020). Symbolic empowerment, a theory of election campaigns involving historic first candidates, goes beyond the traditional Black-white paradigm and considers the impact of multiracial and multiethnic constituencies on American behavioral studies. The goal is: to provide a more comprehensive study of vote choice and election outcomes with support for historic firsts serving as an explanatory variable alongside other sources of variation like political context, geographic space, constituent base, campaign strategy, spending patterns, etc. Given the psychological and social factors linked to identity categories in each context under examination here, researchers and readers alike should come to understand the importance of identity for segments of the mass public that are far from homogenous but rather heterogenous in some of the country's fastest growing areas due to increases in immigration. To be sure, identity alignment between candidates and voters is symbolically empowering and mobilizing for certain populations in especially multicultural urban milieus (Medenica and Fowler 2020). At the same time, the overarching context from which historic firsts emerged onto the political scene in 2018 often referred to as the "Trump era" is analytically important.

The "Trump Era"

Does this symbolic empowerment framework hold in Trump's America? Reflecting on Trump's efforts to target and incorporate a group of motivated previously non-participatory citizens with low level information, misstatements, and distortions is where I begin in terms of defining the overarching context for better understanding recent breakthrough elections (Fording and Schram 2017). Trump supporters, who saw themselves as marginalized and looking for a symbolic candidate outside of the mainstream Washington establishment to empower and alter their political behaviors, could be described in similar terms as supporters of previously marginalized symbolic candidates like Chisholm and Jackson, even as their *privileged* racial status (read: white) overshadows their socioeconomic status and their extremism sets them apart (Fording and Schram 2017). Inspired to appear in our nation's capital on January 6, 2021, to "stop the steal" and alter American presidential election results, they were equally motivated to observe ballot counting, and allege voter fraud. It is not simply a question of whether presidential candidates like Trump bolster political behavior, but the larger question is whether their office seeking as historic firsts stimulates active participation in the selection process (Simien 2015; Simien and Hampson 2020).

The 2016 American presidential election and the "Trump effect" founded on "Making America Great Again" or bringing back the "glory" days of America has proven instructive, as we consider the mobilizing effect of such a ready symbol that made the routine election controversial on account of his hate messaging, racist rhetoric, and emotion-satisfying gestures (Phoenix 2020). Trump's flamboyant style and dramatic oratory resembled a staged performance that conformed to his public persona as an extreme personality, which elicited standing ovations and enthusiastic applause from captive audiences at large public rallies. Over time, Trump benefitted from a shift in perception regarding his viability as a Republican presidential candidate and the spectacle of his 2016 campaign, which was interpreted as actively symbolic by several political analysts who expressed disbelief and raised doubts about his long-term success. While he had no legacy of public service for which to cement his representational ties and affirm his leadership on the main stage of the Republican Party apparatus, he stood before us as a member of the business elite, a real estate developer, and reality television actor. At the same time and, no less importantly, there is perhaps no political office where traditional racial and gender stereotypes worked more to his advantage than the U.S. presidency.

Arguably the "manliest" of all elected offices, the default identity category for the American president has been white *and* male (Duerst-Lahti 2006; Katz 2016). On this basis, Trump could be viewed as best suited for the role of commander-in-chief of the military, overseer of the economy, and country's foremost diplomat in 2016 as opposed to his Democratic opponent, Hillary Clinton, because what it means to be a "woman" in the United States does not correspond well with gendered expectations about what it means to be a "president." While gender does not refer only to women and race does not refer only to Black, the tendency has been to assume that analyzing gender *and* race means focusing on the beliefs, behaviors, treatment, or experiences of women and Black people separate and apart from one another (Simien 2006, 2015). Both the way Trump was presented in the media voluntarily, as a function of his campaign activity, and involuntarily, as a function of political commentary, contributed to his role as an iconoclastic candidate who perpetuated the status quo through his performance of toxic white masculinity (Katz 2016; Dittmar 2017). As such, he reinforced prevailing norms and practices that have long disadvantaged women and constrained men across race and ethnicity in electoral politics. Take, for example, the unique features of his 2016 campaign—specifically, the stylized, repetitive speeches that were direct appeals aimed at arousing emotion among spectators and prospective voters alike. At campaign rallies there were repeated attacks waged against his Democratic opponent, Hillary Clinton, from chants of "Trump that Bitch" and "Lock her Up!" to Donald Trump asking audiences, "Do you think Hillary looks presidential? I don't think so …" (Dittmar 2017).

Once Trump had taken the oath of office and emerged as an incumbent; however, the empowering effect of being a "historic first"—that being, in this case: a Washington outsider with no prior experience as either an office holder or candidate running for political office—had worn off. Republican voters especially those former and present Republicans who established the Lincoln Project sought to prevent his re-election in 2020 and endorsed Democratic presidential nominee, Joe Biden. They were not nearly as inspired by this second campaign especially when he interjected himself into local contests and appeared at numerous rallies for House, Senate, and gubernatorial candidates where he called attention to himself, in effect making himself and his presidency a campaign issue (Cohen 2019; Phoenix 2020). In many districts and statewide contests, Democratic candidates ran against the soon-to-be former president, overtly or more subtly, to mobilize their side and capitalize on what they viewed was negative voter sentiment toward him, resulting in presidential referendum effects that made a difference in determining the "balance of power" between the two major parties in the U.S. House and Senate (Cohen 2019).

Readers must therefore consider how negative feelings toward Trump's first term election resulted in the emergence of newly interested candidates—especially women and racial and ethnic minorities—seeking and winning election to public office in 2018 and 2020 (Dittmar 2017; Lawless and Fox 2018; Brown and Cassese 2020). Take, for example, the Democratic takeover of the U.S. presidency, House of Representatives, and Senate. It affords contributors to this edited volume a remarkable opportunity to build upon the symbolic empowerment framework and provide important insights into several historic campaigns, including those of newly elected Congresswomen of color: U.S. House Representatives Ilhan Omar (D-MN), Ayanna Pressley (D-MA), and Rashida Tlaib (D-MI). Gubernatorial candidate Andrew Gillum of Florida, and mayoral candidate London Breed of San Francisco, CA, are also featured among this line-up of historic firsts who in recent years effectively mobilized American voters across the color line. Not to suggest that intersectionality is shorthand for Black women, but this edited volume has the potential to expand the theoretical capacity of intersectionality research by linking this type of work to the campaigns and elections of historic firsts—namely, U.S. Representatives Omar and Pressley. The edited volume also shores up academic accounts of the mobilizing effect of historic firsts on the American electorate as related to presidential referendum effects writ large.

The number of historic candidates who have been erased from larger political narratives of state and local politics, the U.S. Congress, and presidential elections is astounding. Because of this far—too—frequent occurrence in college and university classrooms as well as high school civics or American government textbooks, the work of this edited book begins by laying the groundwork for future studies of gubernatorial, congressional, and mayoral contests. It leaves readers with a deeper appreciation for historic firsts who have long-standing effects on new segments of the American polity, whether they win or lose, such that "unsuccessful" campaigns have implications for the future of a growing number of historic first candidates seeking public office and desiring increased electoral participation (Simien 2015; Simien and Hampson 2020). Symbolic empowerment transforms an otherwise bleak situation for the better by way of a priming influence. While the candidate's public visibility as it raises the salience of identities—for example, race, ethnicity, and gender shared by the candidate with American voters is important, historic first candidates also want members of their city, state, or home district to recognize them as one of them based on policy interests, not simply their physical characteristics (Mansbridge 1999; Tate 2001, 2003). Given the strong desire to behave in a way that their constituents would be proud—and because they stand to give prominence to issues that otherwise would be ignored—historic first candidates build trust in government institutions (Tate 2003; Reingold 2008; Simien 2015). Such a powerful dynamic whereby historic first candidates are cognizant of their status and understand the process by which they "stand for" dispossessed subgroup members of their constituent base, can revitalize democracy and strengthen its legitimacy by virtue of *both* their presence *and* performance (Pitkin 1967; Phillips 1995; Mansbridge 1999; Young 2000; Dovi 2002).

Members belonging to the same identity group as their representative can "bask in the glory of" the political aspirant's achievements, eliciting a positive intragroup emotion like pride and igniting newfound enthusiasm to actively participate in local, state, and national elections (Marcus, Newman, and MacKuen 2000; Parkison, Fischer, and Manstead 2005; Finn and Glaser 2010; Sullivan 2014). As much as voters want to be substantively represented, they do value descriptive and symbolic representation (Tate 2001, 2003). Whereas descriptive representation is limited to the likeness of candidates in so far as they mirror constituencies based on social or demographic traits, symbolic representation is inclusive of psychological factors that evoke emotions or warm feelings like a sense of pride (Pitkin 1967; Phillips 1995; Tate 2003). The relationship between descriptive and symbolic representation is forged on the campaign trail when historic first candidates elicit positive group-based appraisals of a salient event like their election (Marcus, Newman, and MacKuen 2000; Simien 2015; Simien and Hampson 2017). At the same time and, no less importantly, the barrier-breaking candidate for whom voters identify as "one of them" emerges onto the political scene as a firebrand that sparks their desire to participate in the electoral process. The tentative or conditional terms upon which their candidacies are viewed through the prism of race, gender, and ethnicity fortify the descriptive-symbolic link between political representation and civic engagement, as it becomes evident during the campaign (Pitkin 1967; Mansbridge 1999; Young 2000).

As shown here, one promising way to study historic firsts and symbolic empowerment is to identify illustrative cases that capture the identity alignment between candidates and voters described above. Rather than approach the topic of historic firsts in U.S. elections narrowly by relying exclusively on large-N aggregate data absent an overarching approach, the tie that binds each chapter that follows is the symbolic empowerment framework. The rich diversity between and among cases organized by level of office (gubernatorial, congressional, and mayoral), the political context, spending patterns, geographic space (city, state, or district), constituent base, as well as campaign strategy (deracialization versus identity-based appeals) and the historic nature of the candidate's race, all combine to cumulatively advance said theory.

There are major limitations to large-N data sets, given the lack of variables about local factors that influence election outcomes—for example, respondent attitudes toward the candidates running for office and attributes of the district. Using data from a rich array of primary and secondary sources—voter turnout reports, newspaper coverage, poll data, interviews, and candidate speeches—contributors speak across electoral office—gubernatorial, congressional, and mayoral—to probe the influence of historic firsts and unpack their ground game. Each chapter highlights candidate backgrounds, considering the extent to which their race and gender, class, education, occupation, ideology, and party identification helped or hurt their standing with American voters. Each chapter features basic facts of the campaign while commenting on why the candidate either won or lost their election using the symbolic empowerment framework referenced above. Each chapter answers the following questions: Was there a decisive moment when the candidate pulled ahead or fell behind? Which issues were most important in affecting the electoral behavior of their constituents? Who supported this candidate? Why? Given the historic nature of these campaigns, how do they enhance the influence of women, racial and ethnic minorities, or other underrepresented groups in future elections?

An Overview of the Historic First Candidates: Winners versus Losers

But what about historic first candidates that lose? Americanists have paid too little attention to trailblazing candidacies and their breakthrough elections, including newly emergent candidates who drop out after losing and once the momentum of their campaigns dissipate. Keeping in mind that the original formulation of symbolic empowerment is sensitive to *both* the political contexts *and* an interdependent relationship—that being, in this case between a pioneer cohort followed by their contemporaries—researchers and readers alike must proceed with an acute understanding of the long game when extending the symbolic framework to new cases. While most scholarly work on American elections is results oriented,

I would argue that the "benefits of losing" for historic first candidates are significant and necessary in so far as they pave the way and create the opportunity for future candidates and subsequent victories (Simien 2015). If the possibility of securing office seems remote, conventional wisdom dictates that the time, expense, and risks of a grueling electoral contest make such a venture less gratifying and not worthwhile for most candidates. However, this logic rests on the assumption that securing the office is the only possible benefit of the selection process. It ignores the unexpected performance of such gubernatorial candidates as Stacey Abrams of Georgia and Andrew Gillum of Florida and their ability as historic firsts to promote themselves as a broker, advancing an agenda on behalf of African-American voters and others who historically have been denied the franchise.

Despite being electorally unsuccessful, the spectacle of their respective game-changing performances afforded each the opportunity to acquire experience, prestige, and visibility that neither would have acquired otherwise amongst the voting public, party elites, and political operatives. Surely, we as political scientists as well as the American public can recognize the importance of these historic candidacies despite their losses when thousands of African-American voters were effectively mobilized and newly registered during their respective campaigns. While neither Abrams nor Gillum became governor, the election results indicated the closest of contests and these new historic cases provide an opportunity to examine whether the concept of symbolic empowerment applies to the highest state-level executive office or whether it is a process unique to the Democratic nominating contest for the U.S. presidency. Whereas race, class, and gender often conspire against political activity, Gillum and Abrams breathed new life into these categories by activating symbolic empowerment and at a time when the demographics of these states are changing substantially.

Gillum, who would have been the first Black governor of Florida, was a viable candidate. He received national and international attention because his historic candidacy challenged past notions about where candidates like himself could run competitively and, at the same time, produced tremendous gains in voter turnout. Gillum's gubernatorial race fundamentally altered the national conversation around his electability, having situated Democratic strategists to better understand electoral challenges facing historic first candidates in the state of Florida while also highlighting some remarkable assets in a Republican controlled state.

As Sharon Wright Austin observes in Chapter 2, the study of turnout in the aggregate and across groups by race or partisanship reveals only part of the story. Existing work on race and American elections has traditionally focused on such drivers of turnout, primarily among Black and white voters, as ideology, partisanship, education, and income. Chapter 2, however, contributes to the literature on youth turnout in American elections. CNN national exit poll data are examined alongside Florida statewide voter files over a 20-year period to determine whether voters were more interested in this gubernatorial race because of the historic nature of the campaign and its Black contender, observing along the way the significant increase in voter turnout among young adults (millennials). Considering that young voters emerged as a decisive voting bloc in support of Gillum's historic candidacy, identifying the factors that increase greater electoral participation on the part of young voters will be vitally important for future trailblazing candidates. Although partisanship has long been a prominent feature in state and national politics, understanding how race and partisanship interact to influence youth voter turnout will matter increasingly more in diverse electoral contexts. The historic candidacy of Gillum was unprecedented in Florida and impacted voter turnout in distinct and meaningful ways, as did other path-breaking candidates before him—namely, Governors Deval Patrick of Massachusetts and Douglas Wilder of Virginia.

Similarly, Ilhan Omar's 2018 Congressional victory garnered tremendous national attention for breaking not just one but multiple barriers. Omar became the first Black woman and first woman of color to represent the state of Minnesota in our nation's capital. Born in Somalia, a country in Sub-Saharan Africa, Omar personally experienced the U.S. refugee resettlement process. She is one of a small number of first-generation immigrants serving in the 116th Congress and the first ever African refugee. What explains Omar's historic victory? And how have her distinctive experiences, as a young, hijab-wearing, Black, immigrant woman shaped her leadership and impact as a national elected official? In Chapter 3, Stefanie Chambers and Laurel Elder draw on multiple sources of data to answer these questions and argue that Omar's success had much to do with her ability to distinguish herself from not only the men in the race, but also from other women candidates with identity-based appeals. While the competition played up their past electoral experience, she relied more heavily on two things: values-driven language to emphasize the aspirational direction in which she would like to move public policy, and personal biography to demonstrate her aptitude to hold congressional office due to her relative lack of experience vis-à-vis her opponents.

Ayanna Pressley was also elected in 2018, becoming the first Black woman from Massachusetts to serve in the U.S. House of Representatives and the first person of color to represent its only majority-minority congressional district (which includes three quarters of Boston, and most of Cambridge). While Pressley was no political newcomer to the city of Boston, her campaign garnered widespread media attention on account of her having defeated a ten-term incumbent, Michael Capuano, of the same political party. Given similar policy views made it difficult to differentiate the two candidates, and incumbency remains a powerful barrier to increasing the number of women in Congressional office, such a racially and ethnically diverse district made descriptive and symbolic representation more relevant for the local voting eligible population.

In Chapter 4, Lauren E. Jones and I argue that the electoral context mattered, given the historic nature of the campaign and its mobilizing effect on a racially and ethnically diverse electorate. Neither Capuano nor Pressley could appeal to party alone. Identity-based appeals offered a strategic advantage and were well-received by Democratic voters, given the demographic makeup of the district. Unlike her opponent, she demonstrated the need for a "preferable descriptive representative" like herself whose personal history, experience, and issue positions connect to the district (Dovi 2002). While emphasizing one's qualifications and ability to succeed in office is a priority for all candidates, Pressley had no choice but to rely on values-driven language and identity alignment to defeat the incumbent, Capuano. Emphasizing her race and gender proved to be a smart strategy in an election, where voters were not able to use party as a cue. Although highlighting qualifications and experience was the preferred tactic used by her opponent, it was important for Pressley to choose a strategy that best fit the electoral context. Her identity played a pivotal role in shaping the dynamics of this non-partisan election, where voters were unable to rely on partisanship as a decision-making shortcut and, at the same time, it did not distract from her qualifications and sparked remarkable turnout.

Few would argue that race and gender were the sole factors that determined Pressley's victory or that of U.S. Representative Omar's of Minnesota. There were several other influential factors that interacted and functioned simultaneously that determined the outcome of their congressional elections—for example, the youth vote and record high turnout. How these historic first candidates' race and ethnic identifications affected youth participation, previously inactive voters, and newly registered voters point to the continued significance of Black women in the Democratic Party coalition. There is merit in multiple group identity, given the perspective they bring as Black women to the office and exercise of political leadership. Both high-quality challengers, they skillfully blended mobilization with coalition building in a candidate-centered campaign that targeted underrepresented minorities and immigrant groups in a diverse electoral context. Taken together, the campaigns of representatives Pressley and Omar answer the following questions: How do race *and* gender affect who gets elected, as well as who is voting? What issues do historic first candidates prioritize? Does diversity in electorates make a difference?

In 2018, Rashida Tlaib made history by becoming the first Palestinian American woman elected from Michigan to the U.S. House of Representatives. Her election was a triumph for Arab Americans, Muslim women, and progressive Democrats who wanted to shake up the establishment. While her election provided symbolic empowerment for Arab Americans, Muslims, and women, Tlaib faced a trade-off in having to avoid drawing attention to her identity so not to distract from her qualifications and appeal to the district's majority Black population. Although it is likely that Arab Americans would have voted for a Democrat, it was significant that a Palestinian American candidate who shared their ethnic and religious background was on the ballot. Still, she had to position herself as uniquely qualified to speak about and bring attention to economic justice and environmental protections as a Democratic socialist.

For Tlaib, the strategy that best fit the electoral context was one that emphasized substantive representation over descriptive and symbolic representation for the nation's third poorest district. A crowded field of Black candidates vying to represent a majority Black district, with a small minority of Arab Americans and Muslims, illustrates the necessity for Tlaib to distinguish herself from her opponents who were presumably advantaged by their racial identity. This need for distinctiveness raises important questions about what the candidate chose to emphasize and de-emphasize over the course of the campaign, given the pragmatic need to emerge successful with the demographic majority votes (Collet 2008; McDonald, Porter, and Treul 2020). In Chapter 5, Michael Minta examines her rise to power. Having run a campaign absent identity-based appeals, she emerged triumphant given her fundraising networks, direct mobilization, and political acumen. Possessing the political experience and resources to professionalize her candidacy, Tlaib had the upper hand in elevating herself and the campaign. To what extent were Arab Americans, Muslims, and women symbolically empowered by her 2018 campaign? Using newspaper accounts, bill sponsorships, and participation in committee oversight hearings, this chapter provides a complementary perspective on how legislators' descriptive characteristics—race, ethnicity, or gender—can lead to substantive representation.

In 2018, London Breed won a hotly contested mayoral election, and became the first Black female mayor in San Francisco's 200-year history. If there ever was an election to expect pronounced differences in self-presentation by candidates, it would be in this mayoral election. Given the city's majority white and Asian populations, sparse Black population of about 5 percent, and storied history of LGBTQ activism, the need for this candidate like Tlaib to develop a distinctive self-presentation strategy raises similar questions about what she chose to emphasize and de-emphasize over the course of the campaign. In Chapter 6, Chelsea N. Jones, Crystal Robertson, and Lorrie Frasure examine how Breed faced certain challenges when deciding which traits to focus on, having to distinguish herself not only from her openly gay, white male opponent, but also the Asian woman in the race. Breed played up certain characteristics about herself based on the city's demographics with style, strategy, and message while also positioning herself as uniquely qualified to speak about and bring attention to affordable housing and homelessness (Collet 2008). She successfully compiled the elements of her own personal history, experience, and issue positions using a deracialized campaign strategy to attract the median voter—for example, Breed deftly integrated her standing as a woman and role model for girls. Having to balance racial and ethnic solidarity with the pragmatic need for votes from the city's majority white and Asian populations, she made the best possible case for herself by emphasizing her upbringing, education, notable accomplishments, and connections to the city.

While the extant literature indicates that there may be some advantages to identity-based appeals, it seemed likely that playing up such factors as race and gender would be less advantageous and not the best strategy for this densely populated, metropolitan city of San Francisco or Tlaib's majority-minority district in Michigan. Race and ethnicity may not always be discussed openly throughout a campaign whether it be a mayoral or congressional contest. Breed's historic victory over an Asian woman and an openly gay, white male suggests that she was linguistically and socially adept at demonstrating her ability to attain and succeed in elective office (Collet 2008). The necessity of Breed having to distinguish herself from her opponents who were presumably advantaged by their identities, given a small minority of African-American voters, makes this mayoral contest like Tlaib's congressional race. Neither Breed nor Tlaib were members of the demographic majority. Regardless of background, ambitious candidates like themselves must be strategic and compete for votes across racial and ethnic communities inclusive of foreign-born immigrant and refugee populations. How these historic first candidates chose to present themselves showcases the electioneering techniques that were required of them in comparable electoral environments to be successful, as outgroup members of a demographic majority (Collet 2008; McDonald, Porter, and Treul 2020). Both high-quality challengers, the selective use of language void of identity-based appeals was key to their electoral success. Taken together, the campaigns of Breed and Tlaib answer the following question: How is the race-neutral, deracialization approach shaped by the size of respective groups in each constituency?

Historic Firsts in U.S. Elections takes up the call to think about path-breaking candidates as motivational actors who are uniquely situated in an electoral system that often reifies binary thinking by privileging one axis of identity, either race or gender, not both. Such identity categories as race and gender are not uniformly positioned but situated differently within power hierarchies and shift depending upon the context where differences converge. While it is well understood that race and gender influence the ways in which historic firsts campaign, surprisingly little research exists on how dual, or multiple group identities interact to affect who is mobilized and how voters behave in local, state, and national elections. Arguably, the 2020 elections did not break new and substantial ground for trailblazers as did the 2018 elections. Most significant about 2020 were the gains made in clearing a path to the White House for America's racial and ethnic minorities, and especially women. Even though former presidential candidate, Kamala Harris, secured the office of vice president, the record-high of six female candidates and four men of color who sought the Democratic presidential nomination in 2020, seemed to catalyze the conversation around their electability. To be sure, the Democratic nominating contest was a step forward in this regard and these realistically viable candidates were instrumental in blazing a trail, as did the historic first gubernatorial, congressional, and mayoral candidates featured in the chapters that follow.

Each chapter shows how identity politics is far more complex than recurring "Year of the Woman" or "Race Trumps Gender" frameworks suggest. An array of race-gender similarities and differences are evident in the experiences, activities, and accomplishments of path-breaking candidates; however, it seemed that by all accounts organizationally to mount a "movement campaign," and expand the electoral base through grassroots mobilization was the best strategy for historic first candidates. The major takeaways are clear: the representation of those marginalized by multiple, interlocking systems of power is inextricably tied to the fate of historic first candidates, as was shown by Georgia's 2021 run-off elections for the U.S. Senate, and it has especially important implications for recent voting rights legislation—namely, the For the People Act (H.R. 1) and the John Lewis Voting Rights Act (also known as H.R. 4).

Conclusion

The formulation of symbolic empowerment as a theoretical framework for studying historic first candidates is a major contribution to the American and comparative politics subfields, as evidenced by recent publications—see, for example, Alexander and Jalalzai 2020; Simien and Hampson 2020. Still, this edited volume is the first of its kind. As such, it is exploratory in nature rather than definitive in its empirical testing of this theoretical concept. While *both* probing the generality of past findings *and* recognizing the difficulties of establishing equivalence among electoral contexts, the symbolic empowerment framework helps researchers establish sufficiently similar patterns for which to evaluate new cases and adapt them to "fit" for comparative purposes. I, along with the contributors of this volume, spotlight different ways of approaching historic candidacies using a relational approach to analyze cases, both normatively and empirically. It is our hope that future researchers will pick up where we have left off, with this being the first of many such works to introduce a range of cases and expand the reach of symbolic empowerment beyond the Trump era. Being mindful of the overarching context from which these historic firsts emerged onto the political scene in 2018 is analytically important.

Future research might consider a larger set of cases that vary by gender, race, ethnicity, and time simultaneously, so commonalities and differences can be systematically coded and problematized, but *without* distorting the symbolic empowerment framework using a large-N approach. The result might yield secondary categories that differentiate between winners and losers, establish a pioneer cohort in relation to contemporaries, or identify some partial cases that fail to symbolically empower. Indeed, for every Ilhan Omar or Ayanna Pressley, there are surely other candidates like Gillum who achieved identity alignment with segments of the mass public but failed to win election. Adding new cases to make credible claims about both the complexity and importance of historic first candidates at the level of state, local, and national government can only enhance our current understanding of symbolic empowerment, as would interest in its utility beyond the United States. Whether variations in application or meaning as well as categorization are accepted or contested will be an abiding issue for future research.

References

Alexander, Amy C., and Farida Jalalzai. 2020. "Symbolic Empowerment and Female Heads of States and Government: A Global, Multilevel Analysis." *Politics, Groups, and Identities* 8(1): 24–43.

Brown, Nadia E., and Erin C. Cassese. 2020. "The Role of Gender in the 2018 Midterm Elections." *Political Research Quarterly* 73(4): 923–925.

Burge, Camille D. 2020. "Black Affective Experiences in Politics," *Politics, Groups, and Identities* 8(2): 390–395.

Castle, Jeremiah J., Shannon Jenkins, Candice D. Ortbals, Lori Poloni-Staudinger, and J. Cherie Strachan. 2020. "The Effect of the #Me Too Movement on Political Engagement and Ambition in 2018." *Political Research Quarterly* 73(4): 926–941.

Center for American Women and Politics (CAWP). 2018. "Results: Women Candidates in the 2018 Elections." New Brunswick, NJ: Eagleton Institute of Politics, Rutgers, the State University of New Jersey.

Cohen, Jeffrey E. 2019. "Presidential Referendum Effects in the 2018 Midterm Election: An Initial Analysis." *Presidential Studies Quarterly* 49(3): 669–683.

Collet, Christian. 2008. "Minority Candidates, Alternative Media, and Multiethnic America: Deracialization or Toggling?" *Perspectives on Politics* 6(4): 707–728.

Dittmar, Kelly. 2017. "Finding Gender in Election 2016: Lessons from Presidential Gender Watch." New Brunswick, NJ: Center for American Women and Politics, Eagleton Institute of Politics, Rutgers, the State University of New Jersey, with the Barbara Lee Family Foundation.

Dovi, Suzanne. 2002. "Preferable Descriptive Representatives: Will Just Any Woman, Black, or Latino Do?" *American Political Science Review* 96(4): 729–743.

Duerst-Lahti, Georgia. 2006. "Presidential Elections: Gendered Space and the Case of 2004." In *Gender and Elections: Shaping the Future of American Politics*, edited by Susan J. Caroll and Richard L. Fox. New York: Cambridge University Press, pp. 12–42.

Epstein, Kayla, and Eugene Scott. 2018. "The Historic Firsts of the 2018 Midterms." *The Fix-The Washington Post*, November 7.

Finn, Christopher, and Jack Glaser. 2010. "Voter Affect and the 2008 U.S. Presidential Election: Hope and Race Mattered." *Analyses of Social Issues and Public Policy* 10(1): 262–275.

Fording, Richard C., and Sanford F. Schram. 2017. "The Cognitive and Emotional Sources of Trump Support: The Case of Low-Information Voters." *New Political Science* 39(4): 670–686.

Hansen, Claire. 2018. "Historic Firsts in the 2018 Midterms." *U.S. News & World Report*, November 13.

Katz, Jackson. 2016. *Man Enough? Donald Trump, Hillary Clinton, and the Politics of Presidential Masculinity.* Northampton, MA: Interlink Publishing Group.

Lawless, Jennifer L., and Richard L. Fox. 2018. "A Trump Effect? Women and the 2018 Midterm Elections." *The Forum* 16(4): 665–686.

Lazarus, Richard. 1991. *Emotion and Adaptation.* New York: Guilford Press.

Levin, Sam, and Julia Carrier Wong. 2018. "A Night of Firsts: The Candidates Who Made History in the 2018 Midterms." *The Guardian*, November 7.

López, Ian Haney. 2015. *Dog Whistle Politics.* New York: Oxford University Press.

Mak, Aaron. 2018. "The Many Historic Firsts from the 2018 Midterms." *Slate,* November 7.

Mansbridge, Jane. 1999. "Should Blacks Represent Blacks and Women Represent Women? A Contingent 'Yes.'" *Journal of Politics* 61(3): 628–657.

Marcus, George E., W. Russell Neuman, and Michael MacKuen. 2000. *Affective Intelligence and Political Judgement.* Chicago, University of Chicago Press.

McDonald, Maura, Rachel Porter, and Sarah A. Treul. 2020. "Running as a Woman? Candidate Presentation in the 2018 Midterms." *Political Research Quarterly* 73(4): 967–987.

Medenica, Vladmimir E., and Matthew Fowler. 2020. "The Intersectional Effects of Diverse Elections on Validated Turnout in the 2018 Midterm Elections." *Political Research Quarterly* 73(4): 988–1003.

Parkison, Brian, Agneta H. Fischer, and Antony S.R. Manstead. 2005. *Emotion in Social Relations: Cultural, Group, and Interpersonal Processes.* New York; Psychology Press.

Pitkin, Hannah. 1967. *The Concept of Representation.* Berkeley and Los Angeles: University of California Press.

Phillips, Anne. 1995. *The Politics of Presence.* New York: Clarendon Press.

Phoenix, Davin L. 2020. The Anger Gap: How Race Shapes Emotion in Politics. New York: Cambridge University Press.

Reingold, Beth, ed. 2008. *Legislative Women: Getting Elected, Getting Ahead.* Boulder, CO: Lynne Rienner Publishers.

Simien, Evelyn M. 2006. *Black Feminist Voices in Politics.* Albany, NY: State University of New York Press.

Simien, Evelyn M. 2015. *Historic Firsts: How Symbolic Empowerment Changes U.S. Politics.* New York: Oxford University Press.

Simien, Evelyn M., and Sarah Cote Hampson. 2017. "Hillary Clinton and the Women Who Supported Her: Emotional Attachments and the 2008 Democratic Presidential Primary." *DuBois Review: Social Science Research on Race* 13(3): 1–24.

Simien, Evelyn M., and Sarah Cote Hampson. 2020. "Black Votes Count, But Do They Matter? Symbolic Empowerment and the Jackson-Obama Mobilizing Effect Across Age and Gender Cohorts." *American Politics Research* 48(6): 725–737.

Sullivan, Gavin Brent, ed. 2014. *Understanding Collective Pride and Group Identity.* New York: Routledge.

Tate, Katherine. 2001. "The Political Representation of Black in Congress: Does Race Matter?" *Legislative Studies Quarterly* 26(4): 623–638.

Tate, Katherine. 2003. *Black Faces in the Mirror.* Princeton, New Jersey: Princeton University Press.

Young, Iris Marion. 2000. *Inclusion and Democracy.* New York: Oxford University Press.

2

ANDREW GILLUM'S QUEST TO BECOME FLORIDA'S FIRST BLACK GOVERNOR

Sharon Wright Austin

After the ratification of the Voting Rights Act of 1965, the increased Black voting registration and turnout resulted a concomitant growth among Black elected officials. Unfortunately, although many African-Americans won local elections, few were elected statewide. In most circumstances, the Black candidate's race was a decisive factor that precluded whites from voting for him or her (Piliawsky 1989, 6). Some white voters even admitted that they would not vote for Black gubernatorial candidates regardless of their qualifications (Jeffries 1999; Jeffries and Jones 2006; Lewis 2010, 179). This coupled with the small Black electorate populations resulted in few serious Black gubernatorial contenders (Jones and Clemons 1993, 129). Only four Black governors have held office in American history. In 1872, Pinckney Benton Stewart Pinchback, a Republican, served as Louisiana's governor for 34 days while incumbent governor, Henry Warmoth, faced impeachment (Harvie 2014). The others were Democrats. More than 100 years after Pinchback served, Virginia Gov. L. Douglas Wilder became the first Black elected governor in the nation's history and served for one four-year term. Other African-American governors include Deval Patrick of Massachusetts (2007–2015) and David Paterson of New York (2008–2010).

In 2018, three African-American candidates—Stacey Abrams of Georgia, Andrew Gillum of Florida, and Ben Jealous of Maryland—competed for their state's highest office. These elections received national and international attention because of the small number of Black gubernatorial contenders over the years and the razor-thin losses of Abrams and Gillum (King 2018). Neither Abrams, Gillum, nor Jealous won their respective races, but their campaigns reaffirmed the abilities of African-American candidates to make serious bids in competitive Southern statewide elections (Dresser 2018). In this chapter, I apply the symbolic empowerment framework to Andrew Gillum's attempt to become Florida's first Black

DOI: 10.4324/9781003213925-2

governor. Mainly, I want to determine the groups that constituted his electoral coalition, whether his presence as a potential "historic first" stimulated Black voter participation in support of his candidacy, and reasons for his loss (Simien 2015).

The Symbolic Empowerment Framework, Data, and Methods

In *Historic Firsts: How Symbolic Empowerment Changes U.S. Politics*, Professor Evelyn Simien (2015) examines the impact of historic figures Shirley Chisholm, Jesse Jackson, Barack Obama, and Hillary Clinton in American presidential elections. She argues that the presence of a "historic first" (a candidate with the ability to become the first of his race, gender, or both in an elective office) "has a mobilizing effect on the marginalized group they represent" (Simien 2015, 11). In other words, voters are more interested in election outcomes when they share an identity with a major contender. Black voters are motivated to participate in these elections because of both the symbolic and substantive benefits they seek to gain from a Black candidate victory (Bobo and Gilliam 1990; Clayton 2010; Simien 2015; Tate 1993; Walters 1988). They also vote in masse for Black presidential candidates because of a shared racial group consciousness that results from their common experiences with racial discrimination and desire to use the political system to address their plight (Austin 2018a).

Symbolic empowerment theory is based on two tenets. First, citizens have higher participation rates when they believe they can determine the election's outcomes. Second, they are more interested in campaigns when they symbolically identify with a candidate from their racial or gender group (Simien 2015, 11, 12). Moreover, Professor Simien discusses the "benefits of losing" as an opportunity for electorally unsuccessful candidates like Chisholm and Jackson to promote themselves as a broker, advancing an agenda on behalf of African-American voters and others who have been denied the franchise (Simien 2015, 133). At the same time and, no less importantly, they pave the way and create the opportunity for future candidates like Hillary Clinton and Barack Obama to emerge as viable candidates and be victorious.

One should not assume that the presence of a Black gubernatorial candidate will automatically spur Black voter turnout or endorsements from Black elected officials, however. In 1982, former Georgia state representative, Mildred Glover, failed to garner significant levels of support from the state's Black officeholders and minimal support from Black voters in her bid to become her state's first Black governor (Walton and Campbell 1994, 245). Professor Raphael Sonenshein (1990) compared Edward W. Brooke's 1966 Massachusetts U.S. Senate campaign with that of Tom Bradley's 1982 California gubernatorial campaign and L. Douglas Wilder's 1985 lieutenant governor's race. He finds that despite the minimal successes of Black statewide candidates, they experience greater prospects for victory when they have political experience, run in states with large white liberal populations, and utilize deracialized campaigns (Sonenshein 1990). However, the experiences of Andrew Young and Tom Bradley as gubernatorial candidates reveal that even Black candidates with "name recognition, media consultants, money, prior campaign experience, powerful connections, [and] editorial support" may fail to win elections (Davis and Willingham 1993, 149; Jeffries and Jones 2006). During the same time that L. Douglas Wilder became Virginia's first Black elected governor, civil rights icon and former congressman, United Nations ambassador, and Atlanta mayor Andrew Young unsuccessfully competed in the 1990 Georgia gubernatorial election. Although the overall turnout was high with over one million voters participating in the election, Young finished second in the Democratic primary (Davis and Willingham 1993, 167).

To answer the chapter's research questions, I summarize the results of exit poll data which are summarized in Tables 2.1–2.4. These data are commonly used in academic research and report interview results from randomly chosen groups of people about their vote choices immediately after they cast their votes (Bolce 1992; Carr 2005). Smaller margins of error are based on larger samples (Carr 2005). Ideally, a poll with a +/−3 percent margin of error is considered as making accurate predictions (Carr 2005). The reliability of polls is also based on the wording of questions and on their sampling error—i.e., the portion of the potential error in a survey introduced by using a sample rather than the entire population (Traugott and Price 1992). Despite problems associated with finding a demographically representative sample, wording questions in an unbiased way, and interviewing procedures, exit poll data usually predict public opinion results accurately (Barreto et al. 2006; Carr 2005; Levy 1983). These data are especially useful in this research because of their assessment of the voting behavior of different racial and ethnic subgroups (Hilmer 2008). I primarily rely upon CNN exit poll results because of their accuracy and diverse samples that adequately reflect the demographics of the areas they study (Cable News Network 2006). Finally, I summarize the gubernatorial data from Florida statewide voter files over a 20-year period that reveal whether voters were more interested in this election because of the presence of a Black contender.

Black Political Clout in Florida

People of Black African descent have always lacked a strong degree of political incorporation in Florida, with incorporation being defined as: (1) the ability of a racial or ethnic group to elect members of its racial group to influential offices and gain influence in a governing coalition that is dominated by the members of their racial or ethnic group (Browning, Marshall, and Tabb 1990, 24); and (2) the degree to which a group has attained "political inclusion" by electing representatives and defeating officeholders who are hostile to their interest (Shefter 1986, 50–51). Even in places like Jacksonville where they were able to elect an African-American mayor (Alvin Brown) in 2011, Black citizens, who constitute about 30 percent of the population there, still lack political power because they have been able to take advantage of their sizable presence in a conservative area that has a history of racial polarization. Moreover, Black voters in Miami-Dade County were initially handicapped by an at-large/nonpartisan system of electing county commissioners and then by a countywide election system for the county mayor and more recently by strong competition from Haitian Americans in commission races.

Two Black men have been appointed as Florida's Secretary of State-Jonathan Clarkson Gibbs II, a presbyterian minister, from 1868 to 1873 and Jesse R. McCrary, an attorney and civil rights activist, for five months in 1978 and 1979 (Florida Department of State 2006–2007). Also, Jennifer Carroll, a Trinidadian-born former Navy officer and only Black female Republican to ever serve in the state legislature, was elected as Lieutenant Governor from 2011 to 2013 during the Rick Scott gubernatorial administration (Carroll 2014; Hooper 2012, 139).

These are the only Black/African-American individuals who have served in statewide offices in Florida, and for several reasons. First, most Black/African-American voters are Democrats in a state dominated by Republicans. The state has not had a Democratic governor since 1998. After the unexpected death of Democratic Governor Lawton Chiles in December 1998, his lieutenant governor, Buddy MacKay, served for 24 days (Coggin 2012; Mackay 2010). Before his death, Governor Chiles was leaving office due to a term limit and Republican John Ellis (Jeb) Bush had already defeated MacKay in the November 1998 gubernatorial election. In 1976, Republicans held only 29 of 120 seats in the Florida House and nine of the 40 seats in the Florida Senate (Moreno and Austin 2015). Currently, Florida Republicans hold 73 of the 120 seats (60 percent) in the House and 23 of the 40 seats (57 percent) in the Senate. Republican majorities have been present in the state senate since 1992 and in the state house of representatives since 1997.

Second, African-Americans have a relatively small statewide population and constitute a majority or a large minority only in a few small Panhandle counties. As of July 1, 2019, the Black population in Florida is estimated to be 16.9 percent (U.S. Census Bureau 2020). This is a 2.3 percent increase from 2000 when Blacks comprised 14.6 percent of Florida's population (Moreno and Austin 2015). African-Americans are the majority of the population in only one county—Gadsden, which has a population of less than 50,000 people. They constitute over 30 percent of the population in only three other small rural counties—Madison (39 percent), Jefferson (36 percent), and Hamilton (34 percent) (Moreno and Austin 2015).

Finally, except for a few predominantly Black municipalities, Black Floridians as a group have failed to gain proportional political representation at the local level. Since the 1990s, over three dozen Black Floridians have been elected to the state legislature. Also, since 1990, nine Blacks (Democrats Corrinne Brown, Val Demings, Alcee Hastings, Al Lawson, Carrie Meek, Kendrick Meek, and Frederica Wilson as well as Republicans Allen West, and Byron Donalds) have been elected to the U.S. House of Representatives (Moreno and Austin 2015).

This most recent success has been a long time coming because of African-Americans' historical underrepresentation in Florida politics. Like the rest of the states of the old Confederacy, the state significantly limited the ability of its African-American citizens to participate in politics. From the end of Reconstruction in 1877 to the advent of the civil rights movement in the 1950s, African-Americans, for all intents and purposes, were shut out of the state's political life. Florida used the Jim Crow legal system of white Democratic primaries, literacy tests, arbitrary methods to determine legal voting age and residency, poll taxes, segregated public facilities, and violence to disenfranchise its African-American citizens (Moreno and Austin 2015). It was not until 1968 that the first Black candidate, John Lang Kershaw of Miami (ironically of Bahamian descent), won election to the Florida Legislature (state house) since Reconstruction (Dunn 1997, 200).

This is in marked contrast with recent Hispanic political ascendancy. Melquiades Rafael Ruiz (Mel) Martinez, a Cuban American Republican, served in the U.S. Senate from 2005 to 2009 and Marco Rubio, also a Cuban American Republican, has served in the U.S. Senate since 2010. In the 2010 election, Kendrick Meek, an African-American Democratic congressman, finished a distant third to Independent Charlie Crist and Republican Marco Rubio. Today, it is nearly impossible to understand Florida politics without considering Hispanic political clout. Florida's role as a swing state in presidential election, combined with the fundraising muscle and bloc voting of Miami's Cuban Americans, the rapid growth of the state's Puerto Rican population along the I-4 corridor, and the growing Central and South American population make the state's Hispanics one of the most influential Latino populations in the United States (Moreno and Austin 2015).

Andrew Gillum's Deracialized Campaign Strategy

During the November 2018 general election, both Andrew Gillum and Ron DeSantis were 39 years old, politically experienced, Florida natives. Former U.S. Rep. Ron DeSantis, who represented Florida's Sixth Congressional District, won his party's nomination by a significant margin. After trailing in the polls for weeks before the Democratic primary election, Gillum, the mayor of Tallahassee, defeated three opponents whose campaign purses exceeded $100 million (Austin 2018a). In a surprising victory, he received a 34.4 percent share of the vote which was almost three points ahead of his closest competitor Gwen Graham (Real Clear Politics 2018). She consistently ranked first in most pre-election day polls because of her achievements, but also the legacy and popularity of her father, former Florida Governor and U.S. Senator Bob Graham. Gillum, the only candidate who was not a millionaire, usually had a third or fourth place ranking. His campaign was encouraged by the two victories of former President Barack Obama, albeit by the close margins of 3.8 percent in 2008 and 0.9 percent in 2012 (Austin 2018a).

Then in 2016, President Trump again put Florida in the Republican category in 2016 by defeating Hillary Clinton by a mere 0.8 percent (Austin 2018b).

To become Florida's first Black governor, Gillum needed to achieve the following. First, his campaign could only be victorious if a large turnout among his base of minority and younger voters came to fruition (Austin 2018a). Second, he needed to expand his appeal among moderate Democrats and Republicans (Austin 2018a). In the primary, he had only won 18 of the state's 67 counties (Austin 2018a). Some of these included counties with larger minority populations like Broward, Miami-Dade, and Palm Beach. He also fared well in some rural or suburban predominantly white counties—like Clay, Escambia, Hendry, and Hamilton (Austin 2018a).

Because Andrew Gillum ran for office in a Southern red state, possessed few funds, and lacked statewide name-recognition, he solicited support from a diverse array of voters through the usage of a deracialized general election campaign. Although Black candidates have won various statewide elections, it has been very difficult for them to convince voters of their viability as gubernatorial candidates. Former Illinois State Comptroller Roland Burris, an African-American former U.S. Senator from Illinois, once referred to Black statewide elected officials as "an endangered species" because of the small number of them (Burris 1985, 3). It is imperative for Black candidates to establish multiracial electoral coalitions because of small Black statewide populations and the unwillingness of some whites to vote for them (Lewis 2010, 179). Only the District of Columbia (50.7 percent) and the states of Mississippi (37.3 percent), Louisiana (32.4 percent), Georgia (32 percent), Maryland (29.4 percent), South Carolina (27.9 percent), Alabama (26.2 percent), North Carolina (21.5 percent), and Delaware (21.4 percent) have Black populations that exceed 20 percent (Anonymous 2017). Although more Black citizens reside in Southern states than any other region, Black statewide candidates have experienced more challenges there, in part, because of the region's complex race relations (Sonenshein 1990, 224).

Unlike in the primaries, the issue of race fared prominently in the general election. Like many other Black candidates using the deracialization strategy, Gillum did not completely avoid racial discussions. This strategy requires that Black candidates de-emphasize racial appeals, but not completely avoid them (Gillespie 2010, 12; McCormick and Jones 1993, 78) Shortly after his primary victory, his opponent Ron DeSantis said, "You know, he is an articulate spokesman for those far-left views and he's a charismatic candidate," but then said, "The last thing we need to do is to monkey this up by trying to embrace a socialist agenda with huge tax increases and bankrupting the state. That is not going to work. That's not going to be good for Florida" (Austin 2018a).

Immediately, a debate surfaced questioning whether the "monkey this up" reference had a racial context. DeSantis later argued that his comment lacked any such meaning, but his critics focused on our nation's ugly practice of equating Black men to monkeys (Hund and Mills 2016). During a debate in October

2018, Gillum discussed DeSantis' decision to speak at conferences hosted by David Horowitz, an anti-Muslim conservative political activist, and said, "First of all, he's got neo-Nazis helping him out in this state. Now, I'm not calling Mr. DeSantis a racist, I'm simply saying the racists believe he's a racist" (Krieg 2018). During the campaign, a white supremacist group sponsored racist robocalls against Gillum in the state, which the DeSantis' campaign disavowed (Dixon 2018). A more troublesome dilemma for Gillum concerned Tallahassee's problems. Three years after he entered office, in June 2017, the FBI began a corruption investigation and subpoenaed city records (Austin 2018a). Gillum eventually paid a $5,000 fine for accepting tickets to see a Broadway play and a boat ride to the Statue of Liberty from a lobbyist (Burlew 2019). During the gubernatorial campaign, the investigation allowed the DeSantis campaign to accuse him of being untrustworthy.

During the Democratic primary and general election cycles, Gillum promised to tackle issues such as criminal justice reform, judicial reform, homelessness, living wages, Medicaid expansion, and universal health care especially for indigent populations (Gancarski 2018). He also continued to emphasize the need for gun control. He had always championed these issues but focused more heavily on the need for gun control after a February 2018 shooting at Marjory Stoneman Douglas High School resulted in the deaths of 17 students and educators in Parkland, Florida. Shortly, after this tragic incident, Gillum led thousands of gun control advocates in a march at Florida State University (Gancarski 2018). He also opposes Florida's controversial 2005 Stand Your Ground Law that allows individuals to endure few or no consequences for using deadly force when defending themselves (Weaver 2008).

The Impact of a Potential Historic Gubernatorial First on Black Voter Participation

After Andrew Gillum's loss, discussions surfaced as to whether he, as a Black candidate, was a victim of the Wilder effect or the Bradley effect. Political scientists have developed two terms, the "Wilder effect" and the "Bradley effect" to describe the disparities between the polling numbers Black candidates receive and their actual vote margins. At times, polls indicate leads, sometimes substantial ones, for Black candidates; yet these candidates either win by the slightest of margins or lose elections (Hopkins 2009, 769). This difference between the expectation and reality for Black candidates has been explained as "subtle biases against black candidates that voters were not willing to voice in polls but that were operative in the voting booth" (Hopkins 2009, 796). According to 1989 polling data, L. Douglas Wilder led his Republican opponent Marshall Coleman by approximately 15 percentage points two weeks before election day, but only won by less than one percent of the vote—that being, approximately 6,700 votes (Hopkins 2009, 769). When former Los Angeles Mayor and African-American candidate, Thomas (Tom) Bradley, competed in the 1982 California gubernatorial election, polls showed him with a considerable lead in the weeks before the November

TABLE 2.1 Polling Results for 2018 Gubernatorial Election

Final Results

Candidate	Gillum	DeSantis	Margin
Total Vote	49.2%	49.6%	0.4%

Polling Predictions

Poll	Date	Sample Size	Margin of Error	Gillum	DeSantis	Predicted Result
RCP Average	10/29–11/5	---------	-------	49.4%	45.8%	Gillum +3.6%
Trafalgar	11/4–11/5	1484	2.5%	47%	50%	DeSantis +3%
St. Pete Polls	11/3–11/4	3088	1.8%	50%	45%	Gillum +5%
Emerson	11/-11/3	748	3.7%	51%	46%	Gillum +5%
HarrisX	10/29–11/4	1400	2.6%	49%	45%	Gillum +4%
Quinnipiac	10/29–11/4	1142	3.5%	50%	43%	Gillum +7%

Source: Real Clear Politics, "All Florida Governor-DeSantis vs. Gillum Polling Data," www.realclearpolitics.com/epolls/2018/governor/fl/florida_governor_desantis_vs_gillum-6518.html, accessed April 20, 2019.

election (Pettigrew and Alson 1988, 12). A few days before the general election, polls predicted that Bradley was "well ahead" of his Republican rival, George Deukmejian, but he lost by a margin of 48.1 percent to 49.3 percent (Pettigrew and Alson 1988, 12). As Table 2.1 reveals, Gillum averaged a 3.6 percent lead, but lost by 0.4 percent in the days before the election. Only one of the six polls had predicted a DeSantis win. In November 2018, Andrew Gillum narrowly lost the election by a margin of 49.6 percent of the vote for Ron DeSantis (4,076,186) to Gillum's 49.2 percent (4,043,723 votes) (Cable News Network 2018).

One can debate the reasons for the inaccurate poll predictions, but the more significant question concerns the impact of his candidacy on Black voters. In recent decades, Democratic candidates have most often been supported by an election coalition of minority, younger, female, and educated voters (García Bedolla and Haynie 2013). On the other hand, white, male, older, rural, and less educated (a high school education or less) voters usually prefer Republican candidates (Giles and Buckner 1993; Sides et al. 2017). According to exit poll data, Gillum received majority voting percentages from candidates who typically vote for Democratic candidates. As shown in Table 2.2, Gillum's campaign was well received by Black men and women. He received 91 percent of the Black male vote and 82 percent of the Black female vote. He also received 31 percent of the white male vote and 47 percent of the white female vote.

Also, as is the case with most Democratic candidates, Gillum received most of the youth vote while older voters preferred his opponent. As Table 2.3 indicates, Florida voters between the ages of 18–29 preferred Andrew Gillum over Ron DeSantis

TABLE 2.2 Racial, Ethnic, and Gender Voter Preferences

	Gillum	*DeSantis*	*No Answer*
White Male	31%	69%	N/A
White Female	47%	51%	2%
Black Male	91%	8%	1%
Black Female	82%	18%	N/A
Others	65%	34%	1%

Source: Cable News Network, "Exit Polls," www.cnn.com/election/2018/exit-polls/florida/ governor, accessed April 8, 2019.

TABLE 2.3 Voter Preferences by Age, Education, and Income in the 2018 Florida Gubernatorial Election

Age	*Gillum*	*DeSantis*	*No Answer*
18–29	61%	37%	2%
30–44	62%	35%	3%
45–64	46%	52%	2%
Over 64	43%	56%	1%

Education	*Gillum*	*DeSantis*	*No Answer*
H.S. or less	44%	53%	3%
Some college	51%	48%	1%
Associate's	47%	51%	2%
Bachelor's	46%	53%	1%
Advanced	57%	42%	1%

Income	*Gillum*	*DeSantis*	*No Answer*
Under $30,000	63%	39%	1%
$30,000–$49,999	49%	51%	N/A
$50,000–$99,999	52%	47%	1%
$100,000–$199,999	50%	50%	N/A
$200,000 or more	N/A	N/A	N/A

Source: Cable News Network, "Exit Polls," www.cnn.com/election/2018/exit-polls/florida/governor, accessed April 8, 2019.

by a margin of 61 percent to 37 percent while those between the ages of 30 to 44 preferred Gillum over DeSantis by a margin of 62 percent to 35 percent. However, 52 percent of voters between the ages of 45 to 64 and 56 percent of voters of the age of 65 and older preferred DeSantis. Even though most middle-aged and older voters preferred the DeSantis campaign, Gillum still fared well with these voters by receiving 46 percent and 43 percent, respectively, from voter in these age ranges.

Concerning the education and income results in Table 2.3, voters with a high school education or less preferred Ron DeSantis (53 percent) while those with

TABLE 2.4 Voter Preferences by Partisan and Ideological Affiliation

Party Identification	Gillum	DeSantis	No Answer
Democrats (33%)	93%	7%	N/A
Republicans (38%)	7%	92%	1%
Independents (29%)	54%	44%	2%

Ideology	Gillum	DeSantis	No Answer
Liberal (22%)	90%	9%	1%
Moderate (39%)	61%	38%	1%
Conservative (39%)	13%	85%	2%

Source: Cable News Network, "Exit Polls," www.cnn.com/election/2018/exit-polls/florida/governor, accessed April 8, 2019.

advanced degrees preferred Andrew Gillum (57 percent). In addition, voters earning incomes of $30,000 or less and between $50,000 and $99,999 favored the Gillum campaign (63 percent and 52 percent, respectively). However, voters earning incomes between $100,000 and $199,999 split their votes between Gillum and DeSantis with each earning 50 percent of their votes.

According to Table 2.4, the greatest polarization was along ideological and partisan lines. Voters classifying themselves as liberals preferred Gillum by a 90 percent margin over his opponent while 61 percent of moderates voted for his campaign. Voters with conservative ideologies voted for DeSantis by a margin of 85 percent. In addition, well over 90 percent of Democratic and Republican voters, respectively, cast their support based on partisanship. Gillum received a strong backing from the local, state, and national chapters of the Democratic Party. Thus, this was not a case in which white citizens voted across partisan lines rather than vote for a candidate of color (Skinner and Klinkner 2004).

Did Andrew Gillum's emergence as potentially Florida's Black governor result in increased Black voter support and decreased white voter support? To answer this question, I observe data in Table 2.5 that reveal a racial breakdown of votes received by Democratic and Republican gubernatorial candidates dating back to 1998. The Gillum electoral coalition consisted of people of African descent (86 percent), Hispanics (54 percent), and whites (39 percent). Florida's Democratic candidates usually receive white voting percentages in the high 30- and low 40-percentile range. In addition, Gillum's 86 percent Black vote was like the high 89-percentile/low 90-percentile margins received by Democratic candidates. However, his 86 percent Black vote was lower than the 94 percent received by white male Democratic candidate Bill McBride in 2002, the 92 percent by white female Democratic candidate Alex Sink in 2010, and the 88 percent received by former Florida Governo Charlie Crist in 2014. Crist ran for governor as both a

TABLE 2.5 Voting Results for Florida Gubernatorial Candidates by Race, 1998–2014

Candidate	Black	White	Hispanic	Candidate	Black	White	Hispanic
1998				*2002*			
*Jeb Bush (R.-FL)	14%	60%	61%	*Jeb Bush (R.-FL)	6%	59%	60%
Buddy Mackay (D.-FL)	86%	40%	39%	Bill McBride (D.-FL)	94%	41%	40%
2006				*2010*			
*Charlie Crist (R.-FL)	18%	59%	49%	*Rick Scott (R.-FL)	6%	56%	50%
Jim Davis (D.-FL)	81%	38%	49%	Alex Sink (D.-FL)	92%	41%	48%
2014				*2018*			
*Rick Scott (R.-FL)	12%	46%	38%	Ron DeSantis (R.-FL)	14%	60%	44%
Charlie Crist (D.-FL)	88%	39%	58%	Andrew Gillum (D.-FL)	86%	39%	54%

Sources: Charles S. Bullock III and Mark J. Rozell, eds., *The New Politics of the Old South: An Introduction to Southern Politics* (Lanham, MD: Rowman and Littlefield 2014), 61; New York Times, "Election 2010," www.nytimes.com/elections/2010/results/governor/exit-polls.html; accessed April 10, 2020; Douglas C. Lyons, "Did Black Voters Deliver for Rick Scott," *South Florida Sun Sentinel* November 10, 2014, www.sun-sentinel.com/opinion/todays-buzz/sfl-did-black-voters-deliver-for-rick-scott-20141110-story.html, accessed April 29, 2020; Jens Manuel Krogstad and Mark Hugo Lopez, "Hispanic Voters in the 2014 Election," *Pew Research Center Hispanic Trends* November 7, 2014, www.pewresearch.org/hispanic/2014/11/07/hispanic-voters-in-the-2014-election/, accessed April 9, 2020; Cable News Network, "Exit Polls," www.cnn.com/election/2018/exit-polls/florida/governor, accessed April 8, 2019.

* Winner of the election

Democrat and Republican in two separate elections. The 14 percent Black vote received by Ron DeSantis (and the 14 percent received by Jeb Bush in 1998) was the second highest percentage of Black votes received by a Republican since 1998. In 2006, Charlie Crist received an 18 percent Black voting margin. Historically in Florida, most Hispanic voters have supported Republicans. Since 1998, only Andrew Gillum (54 percent) and Charlie Crist (58 percent in 2014) received larger shares of Hispanic votes than Republican candidates. Therefore, Andrew Gillum's campaign enabled him to establish solid multiracial electoral coalitions. Despite this, he lost because of the turnout factor.

Table 2.6 summarizes the turnout rates and candidate total vote percentages in Florida gubernatorial elections over a 20-year period. This turnout (63 percent) was higher than it had been in previous gubernatorial elections. Scholarly research has discovered that general turnout rates are higher when credible Black statewide candidates are competing (Atkins 1985; Washington 2006).

TABLE 2.6 Election Turnout in Florida Gubernatorial Election, 1998–2018

Election Year	Overall Turnout	Republican Nominee	Democrat Nominee
1998	49%	*Jeb Bush (55.3%)	Buddy Mackay (44.7%)
2002	55%	*Jeb Bush (56%)	Bill McBride (43.1%)
2006	47%	*Charlie Crist (52.1%)	Jim Davis (45.1%)
2010	49%	*Rick Scott (48.8%)	Alex Sink (47.7%)
2014	51%	*Rick Scott (48.1%)	Charlie Crist (47%)
2018	63%	*Ron DeSantis (49.5%)	Andrew Gillum (49.1%)

Sources: Florida Division of Elections, "Voter Turnout," https://dos.myflorida.com/elections/data-statistics/elections-data/voter-turnout/, accessed April 29, 2020; U.S. Election Atlas, "Gubernatorial General Election Results Comparison-Florida," https://uselectionatlas.org/RESULTS/compare.php?year=1998&fips=12&f=0&off=5&elect=0&type=state, accessed April 23, 2020.

* Winner of the election. Numbers are given for both the general and runoff election.

Conclusion

In 2018, Andrew Gillum became one of the few African-American serious contenders in a gubernatorial election. Throughout American history, such campaigns have been rare. It remains difficult for Black candidates to present themselves as possible chief executives of states. Andrew Gillum lost the election primarily because of his inability to attract the levels of turnout necessary to ensure a victory. It is unclear whether the endorsements of Donald Trump for Republican candidates or those of Barack Obama and celebrities, such as Oprah Winfrey, influenced Democratic or Republican turnout more significantly. However, Gillum would have won if the turnout rates among the members of his electoral coalition had been higher.

Two Black statewide elected officials, U.S. Senator Edward Brooke and Virginia Governor L. Douglas Wilder, discussed the qualities Black candidates need to win statewide elections. These include, first, "serving an appropriate political apprenticeship" (Jeffries 1999, 584; Jeffries 2000). Before seeking a statewide office, Black candidates should have held at least one elective office, preferably at the state level. Second, they must have name recognition because of their distinguished public service. Third, they must have won the election they held immediately before they rank for office (Jeffries 1999, 584). Individuals who hold offices such as mayoral and state or national representative usually have not served in the kinds of offices Brooke and Wilder discussed (Jeffries 1999, 584). Fourth, these candidates must conduct deracialized campaigns because they are seeking office in predominantly white environments (Jeffries 1999, 584). Finally, Black candidates must have the "enthusiastic" support of a major party because of their needs for financial and other resources (Jeffries 1999, 585). When applying this framework to the Andrew Gillum campaign, it is apparent that he was qualified; yet it is debatable whether he had an adequate political apprenticeship prior to running for governor.

What can we gather from these results? Even when candidates use deracialized messages to mobilize the masses against elites, Southern gubernatorial elections remain racially polarized. Also, Gillum received more crossover votes from white voters than DeSantis did from Black voters. This fact confirms that Black voters cast more cohesive bloc votes than white voters, especially when a Black gubernatorial candidate is present (Bullock 1984; Schexnider 1990). Regardless of their race, Democratic candidates face uphill battles when seeking gubernatorial offices in the South because of the dominance of Republican governors there. Currently, Louisiana and North Carolina are the only two states in the deep South with Democratic governors while Arkansas, Tennessee, Texas, Mississippi, Oklahoma, Alabama, Georgia, Florida, and South Carolina are governed by Republicans (Kondik 2018). Liberal candidates possess the ability to develop strong multiracial electoral coalitions which bodes well for statewide minority candidates in a demographically changing South. However, his campaign also indicates that every vote counts in determining the outcomes of competitive elections.

References

Anonymous. 2017. "Ten States with the Largest African-American Populations." *World Atlas* April 25. www.worldatlas.com/articles/us-states-with-the-largest-relative-african-american-populations.html. Accessed on April 9, 2019.

Atkins, Burton, Matthew R. DeZee, and William Eckert. 1985. "The Effect of a Black Candidate in Stimulating Voter Participation in Statewide Elections: A Note on a Quiet 'Revolution' in Southern Politics." *Journal of Black Studies* 16(2): 213–225.

Austin, Sharon D. Wright. 2018a "Could Andrew Gillum Be the Next Governor of Florida?" *The Conversation,* August 31, 2018. https://theconversation.com/could-andrew-gillum-be-the-next-governor-of-florida-102451. Accessed on August 31, 2018.

Austin, Sharon D. Wright. 2018b. *The Caribbeanization of Black Politics: Race, Group Consciousness, and Political Participation in America.* Albany, NY: State University of New York Press.

Barreto, Matt A., Fernando Guerra, Mara Marks, Stephen A. Nuno, and Nathan D. Woods. 2006. "Controversies in Exit Polling: Racially Stratified Homogenous Precinct Approach." *PS: Political Science and Politics* 39(3): 477–483.

Bobo, Lawrence, and Franklin Gilliam Jr. 1990. "Race, Sociopolitical Participation, and Black Empowerment." *American Political Science Review* 82(2): 377–393.

Bolce, Louis, Gerald De Maio and Douglas Muzzio. 1992. "Blacks and the Republican Party: The 20 Percent Solution." *Political Science Quarterly* 107(1): 63–79.

Browning, Rufus, Dale Rogers Marshall, and David Tabb. 1990. "Minority Mobilization in Ten Cities. Failures and Successes." In *Racial Politics in American Cities.* 1st Edition, eds. Rufus P. Browning, Dale Rogers Marshall, and David H. Tabb. New York: Longman, 8–30.

Bullock, Charles S. 1984. "Racial Crossover Voting and the Election of Black Officials." *The Journal of Politics* 46(1): 238–251.

Burlew, Jeff. 2019. "Andrew Gillum Settles Ethics Case, Agrees to $5,000 Fine." *Tallahassee Democrat*, April 24, 2019. www.tallahassee.com/story/news/local/fbi/2019/04/24/andrew-gillum-ethics-hearing-delayed-until-11-a-m/3538733002/. Accessed on April 27, 2020.

Burris, Roland. 1985. "Winning Statewide Office." *Focus* 13 (October): 3.

Carr, Deborah. 2005. "Primer: Political Polls." *Contexts* 4(1): 31–32.

Carroll, Jennifer L. 2014. *When You Get There: An Autobiography*. Charleston, SC: Advantage Media Group.

Cable News Network. 2006. "America Votes 2006: Project Explainer." www.cnn.com/ELECTION/2006/pages/results/misc/projected.html. Accessed on April 10, 2020.

Cable News Network. 2018. "Live Election Results: Florida." www.cnn.com/election/2018/results/florida/governor. Accessed on April 8, 2019.

Clayton, Dewey M. 2010. *The Presidential Campaign of Barack Obama: A Critical Analysis of a Racially Transcendent Strategy*. New York: Routledge.

Coggin, John Dos Passos. 2012. *Walkin' Lawton*. Cocoa, FL: The Florida Historical Society Press.

Davis, Marilyn, and Alex Willingham. 1993. "Andrew Young and the Georgia State Elections in 1990." In *Dilemmas of Black Politics: Issues of Leadership and Strategy*, ed. Georgia A. Persons. New York: Harper Collins College Publishers, 146–175.

Dixon, Matt. 2018. "Gillum Ties DeSantis to Racist Robocalls Day After Asking They Receive No 'Attention.'" *Politico,* October 24, 2018. www.politico.com/states/florida/story/2018/10/24/gillum-ties-desantis-to-racist-robocalls-day-after-asking-they-receive-no-attention-663730. Accessed on April 27, 2019.

Dresser, Michael. 2018. "Jealous, Gillum, Abrams Call for New Playbook in Majority-White States." *Baltimore Sun,* September 13, 2018. www.baltimoresun.com/news/maryland/politics/bs-md-jealous-nominees-20180913-story.html. Accessed on April 29, 2019.

Dunn, Marvin. 1997. *Black Miami in the Twentieth*. Gainesville, FL: University Press of Florida.

Florida Department of State. 2006–2007. "Secretary of State Office History." https://web.archive.org/web/20071016114731/http://oss.dos.state.fl.us/history.cfm. Accessed on May 20, 2020.

Gancarski, A.G. 2018. "Andrew Gillum, Backed by Billionaires, Delivers Populist Sermon in Jacksonville." *Florida Politics,* July 6, 2018. https://floridapolitics.com/archives/268090-gillum-jax. Accessed on April 16, 2019.

García Bedolla, Lisa, and Kerry L. Haynie. 2013. "The Obama Coalition and the Future of American Politics." *Politics, Groups, and Identities* 1(1): 128–133.

Giles, Michael W., and Melanie A. Buckner. 1993. "David Duke and Black Threat: An Old Hypothesis Revisited." *The Journal of Politics* 55(3): 702–713.

Gillespie, Andra. 2010. *Whose Black Politics? Cases in Post-Racial Black Leadership*. New York: Routledge Press.

Harvie, Maureen. 2014. "Why Have There Been So Few Black Governors." *WYPR News,* June 5, 2014. http://news.wypr.org/post/why-have-there-been-so-few-black-governors#stream/. Accessed on April 13, 2019.

Hilmer, Richard. 2008. "Exit Polls—A Lot More Than Just a Tool for Election Forecasts." In *Public Opinion Polling in a Globalized World*, eds. Marita Carballo and Ulf Hjelmar. New York: Springer, 93–108.

Hooper, Cindy. 2012. *Conflict: African American Women and the New Dilemma of Race and Gender in Politics*. New York: Praeger.

Hopkins, Daniel J. 2009. "No More Wilder Effect, Never a Whitman Effect: When and Why Polls Mislead about Black and Female Candidates." *The Journal of Politics* 71(3): 769–781.

Hund, Wulf D., and Charles W. Mills. 2016. "Comparing Black People to Monkeys Has a Long, Dark Simian History." *The Conversation,* February 28, 2016. https://theconve rsation.com/comparing-black-people-to-monkeys-has-a-long-dark-simian-history-55102. Accessed on April 27, 2019.

Jeffries, Judson L. 1999. "U.S. Senator Edward W. Brooke and Governor L. Douglas Wilder Tell Political Scientists How Blacks Can Win High-Profile Statewide Office." *PS: Political Science and Politics* 32(3): 583–588.

Jeffries, Judson L. 2000. *Virginia's Native Son: The Election and Administration of Governor L. Douglas Wilder*. West Lafayette, IN: Purdue University Press.

Jeffries, Judson L., and Charles E. Jones. 2006. "Blacks Who Run for Governor and the U.S. Senate: An Examination of Their Candidacies." *The Negro Educational Review* 57 (2006): 243–261.

King, Shaun. 2018. "Andrew Gillum, Stacey Abrams, and Ben Jealous Could Be the First Black Governors of their States. Here's They How Got This Far." *The Intercept,* August 28, 2018. https://theintercept.com/2018/08/29/andrew-gillum-stacey-abrams-ben-jealous-black-governors/. Accessed on April 29, 2019.

Kondik, Kyle. 2018. "Governors 2019-2020: Democrats Try to Hold the Line in Red-State Battles." *Rasmussen Reports,* December 6. www.rasmussenreports.com/public_con tent/political_commentary/commentary_by_kyle_kondik/governors_2019_2020_ democrats_try_to_hold_the_line_in_red_state_battles. Accessed on April 9, 2019.

Krieg, Gregory. 2018. "Andrew Gillum on DeSantis: 'The Racists Believe He's a Racist.'" *CNN Politics.* October 25. www.cnn.com/2018/10/24/politics/andrew-gillum-ron-desantis-debate-race-hamilton/index.html. Accessed on April 27, 2019.

Levy, Mark R. 1983. "The Methodology and Performance of Election Day Polls." *Public Opinion Quarterly* 47: 54–67.

Lewis, Angela K. 2010. "Between Generations: Deval Patrick's Election as Massachusetts' First Black Governor." In *Whose Black Politics? Cases in Post-Racial Black Leadership*, ed. Andra Gillespie. New York: Routledge, 177–194.

MacKay, Buddy. 2010. *How Florida Happened: The Political Education of Buddy MacKay.* Gainesville, FL: University Press of Florida.

McCormick II, Joseph P., and Charles E. Jones. 1993. "The Conceptualization of Deracialization: Thinking Through the Dilemma." In *Dilemmas of Black Politics: Issues of Leadership and Strategy*, ed. Georgia A. Persons. New York: Harper Collins, 66–84.

Moreno, Dario, and Sharon D. Wright Austin. 2015. "Politics and Ethnic Change in Florida." Unpublished Document.

Pettigrew, Thomas F., and Denise A. Alston. 1988. *Tom Bradley's Campaigns for Governor: The Dilemma of Race and Political Strategies*. Washington, DC: Joint Center for Political Studies.

Piliawsky, Monte. 1989. "Racial Politics in the 1988 Presidential Election." *The Black Scholar* 20(1): 30–37.

Real Clear Politics. 2018. "2018 Florida Governor-Republican Primary-Final Results." www.realclearpolitics.com/epolls/2018/governor/Florida.html. Accessed on April 28, 2019.

Schexnider, Alvin J. 1990. "The Politics of Pragmatism: An Analysis of the 1989 Gubernatorial Election in Virginia." *PS: Political Science and Politics* 23(2): 154–156.

Shefter, Martin. 1986. "Political Incorporation and the Extrusion of the Left: Party Politics and Social Forces in New York City." *Studies in American Political Development* 1 (Spring): 50–90.

Sides, John, Michael Tesler, and Lynn Vavreck. 2017. "The 2016 U.S. Election: How Trump Lost and Won." *Journal of Democracy* 28(2): 34–44.

Simien, Evelyn M. 2015. *Historic Firsts: How Symbolic Empowerment Changes U.S. Politics* New York: Oxford University Press.

Skinner, Richard, and Philip A. Klinkner. 2004. "Black, White, Brown, and Cajun: The Racial Dynamics of the 2003 Louisiana Gubernatorial Election." *The Forum* 2(1): 1–8.

Sonenshein, Raphael. 1990. "Can Black Candidates Win Statewide Elections?" *Political Science Quarterly* 105(2): 219–241.

Tate, Katherine. 1993. *From Protest to Politics: The New Black Voters in American Elections.* Cambridge: Harvard University Press.

Traugott, Michael W., and Vincent Price. 1992. "A Review: Exit Polls in the 1989 Virginia Gubernatorial Election." *Public Opinion Quarterly* 56(2): 245–253.

U.S. Census Bureau. 2020. "Quick Facts. Florida." www.census.gov/quickfacts/FL. Accessed on May 20, 2020.

Walters, Ronald W. 1988. *Black Presidential Politics in America: A Strategic Approach.* Albany, NY: State University of New York Press.

Walton, Hanes Jr., and Johnny Campbell Jr. 1994. "The First Black Gubernatorial Candidate in Georgia: State Representative Mildred Glover." In *Black Politics and Black Political Behavior: A Linkage Analysis*, ed. Hanes Walton Jr. Westport, CT: Praeger, 235–250.

Washington, Ebonya. 2006. "How Black Candidates Affect Voter Turnout." *The Quarterly Journal of Economics* 121(3): 973–998.

Weaver, Zachary L. 2008. "Florida's 'Stand Your Ground Law': The Actual Effects and the Need for Clarification." *University of Miami Law Review* 63(1): 395–430.

3

ILHAN OMAR

Breaking Barriers for Muslim, Somali American, and Immigrant Women

Stefanie Chambers and Laurel Elder

Ilhan Omar's 2018 Congressional victory garnered tremendous national attention for breaking not just one but multiple barriers. In January 2019, when she was sworn in as the U.S. Representative from the 5th Congressional District in Minnesota, Ilhan Omar, along with Rashida Talib of Michigan, became the first Muslim woman ever to serve in Congress. Omar also became the first member of Congress to wear a hijab on the floor of the House, a historic first that required the overturning of a 181-year ban on head coverings of any type in the House chamber. Omar was also the first Black woman and first woman of color to represent the state of Minnesota in the nation's capital. Born in Somalia, a country in Sub-Saharan Africa, Omar personally experienced the U.S. refugee resettlement process. She is one of a small number of first-generation immigrants serving in the 116th Congress and the first ever African refugee (Geiger 2019). Omar brings other underrepresented perspectives to her work in Congress as well. She was 36 years old when she entered Congress, more than two decades younger than most of her colleagues (Congressional Research Service 2019). She is also the mother of young children, which remains an uncommon experience among women in the national legislature (Congressional Research Service 2019).

What explains Ilhan Omar's historic Congressional victory? And how have her distinctive experiences, as a young, hijab-wearing, Black, immigrant woman shaped her leadership and impact as a national elected official? In this chapter, we draw on multiple sources of data to answer these questions including news coverage from the Twin Cities' major newspaper,[1] analysis of Congresswoman Omar's newsletters, demographic, and political information about the Congressional district she represents, and importantly, original in-depth interviews with Somali Americans living in Minnesota and in her congressional district. We argue that a key ingredient of Omar's success has been her ability to draw on the multiple

DOI: 10.4324/9781003213925-3

path-breaking dimensions of her identity to assemble, inspire, and empower a diverse electoral coalition to become civically engaged.

Further, we draw on scholarship exploring the intersection of women's representation and party polarization to place Omar's congressional victory in a broader context, arguing that her ability to influence legislation, like most women of color, is very much tied to the fate of the Democratic Party (Elder 2021). Omar and her progressive colleagues also face opposition from a Republican party in Congress that has become even more dominated by white men over the past several election cycles (Elder 2020) and is led in the White House by a President who has drawn on sexist, racist, and anti-immigrant sentiments to win office and maintain support (Brewer and Dundes 2018; Hooghe and Dassonville 2018; Wong 2019). After the remarkable 2018 elections of Congresswomen Ilhan Omar, Rashida Talib, Ayanna Pressley, and Alexandria Ocasio-Cortez, a group collectively known as "the squad," attention to these four freshman members of Congress has been constant. Their diversity and progressive politics in a time of partisan polarization and the nativist rhetoric of President Trump has helped make these women household names. Omar's outspoken criticism of Trump, and his personalized, Islamophobic, and xenophobic reactions as well as the backlash she has faced from President Trump and his allies illustrate both the vitally important role and the daunting challenges faced by the diverse group of women serving in the 116th Congress.

Understanding Omar's political trajectory and against-the-odds success in politics is both inspiring and instructive for scholars, activists, potential candidates, and citizens who do not reflect the traditional older, white, male membership of Congress, as well as those concerned with the rise of racist and anti-immigrant sentiments in American life. We argue that Omar's political campaigns and membership in Congress have sparked interest, civic engagement, and political confidence among marginalized communities in the Unites States who, prior to Omar's election, had never seen someone who looked like them in the highest levels of political power. We conclude the chapter by examining the ways Omar's success appears to have motivated and inspired more young people, immigrants, Muslim women, and Somali Americans to become engaged in the political process.

From African Refugee to the First Somali American State Legislator

Among the many ways Ilhan Omar represents an historic first in American electoral politics is that she was the first Somali American elected to state legislative office, not just in Minnesota but in the United States. She was born in Somalia in 1982. When Omar was eight years old, her family fled the civil war there and moved to the neighboring country of Kenya, where her family lived for four years in a refugee camp. After being sponsored for asylum, the family moved to the United States and eventually settled in Minneapolis, Minnesota (Witt 2018).

Omar showed an interest in politics from a young age. As a young teen, she regularly attended Democratic Party events with her grandfather to translate for him, an experience which piqued her interest in political activism and fostered a desire to have an impact.[2] In 2000, at the age 17, Ilhan Omar became an American citizen (Forliti 2018). Omar graduated from University of North Dakota, where she majored in political science. She then returned to Minnesota to work on public health outreach (Witt 2018). She began getting more involved in local politics, volunteering her time whenever possible for the Democratic Party and other progressive organizations. In 2013, she became a senior policy aide to Minneapolis City Council member Andrew Johnson, and then became director of policy initiatives at Women Organizing Women (Bierschbach and Hirsi 2016).

One unusual aspect of Omar's political ascendance is that she began her electoral career defeating a long serving incumbent within her own party. Omar's first bid for elective office was for a seat in the Minnesota state legislature to represent District 60B, a heavily Democratic district covering a portion of the capital city, Minneapolis. Given the massive incumbency advantage in the U.S. political system in both state legislatures and Congress, the best opportunities for entering office are through open seats (Darcy, Clark, and Welch 1994; Tate 1997). Yet Omar did not wait to run until a state legislative seat opened. Rather, Omar challenged and ultimately defeated Phyllis Kahn, a 22-term incumbent, as well as another challenger, Mohamud Noor, in the Democratic primary. According to Somali Americans living in Minnesota at this time, Omar's victory in the Democratic state legislative primary stemmed from the mobilization of several important constituencies who felt symbolically empowered by her campaign: college students from the University of Minnesota, who have traditionally low turnout, progressive whites, and East African immigrants. One respondent explained:

> In her house district victory, she expanded the electorate by focusing on the most vulnerable and underserved electorate in her district—college students. She got more college students to register and vote for the first time. There were several hundred college students who helped her win. Then she galvanized the progressive organizations and got them to support her candidacy. That helped take away from the incumbent or establishment vote. Then she went and used her Somali card to get more East Africans to vote. So, by being this strategic, that's how she was able to win.
>
> *Community interview 10/31/2019*

As referenced in this quote, Omar's candidacy appealed to East African Immigrants, particularly Somali Americans. Contrary to what some might expect, research shows that Somali Americans participate in Democratic politics at a rate that exceeds many racial and ethnic minorities in the United States (Chambers 2017).

Because Omar established herself as a vocal advocate for underserved groups and raised awareness of specific challenges faced by Somalis and other Muslims, her support in that community was substantial. One Somali respondent in this study said:

> We (Somalis) would have gone to vote in that election regardless of who was running. But I would say here was more excitement because someone we knew, who had been advocating for us and who understood us, was running. And the campaign work done by Somali Americans (for Omar) was also very important to her campaign. I would say that more Somali women participated in her campaign than any other.
>
> *Community interview 4/14/2020*

The ability of Omar to appeal to a broad constituency in her first electoral bid set the stage for more electoral victories.

After winning the primary, Omar went on to easily win the general election against the Republican candidate, Abdimalik Askar, who like Omar was a politically active member of Minnesota's Somali American community. Thus, in January 2017, when she was sworn in, Omar became the first Somali American state legislator in Minnesota and in the entire United States (Herrera and Majerle 2018).

Symbolic Empowerment and a Winning Congressional Coalition

Omar filed to run for Congress, to represent Minnesota's 5th Congressional District, in June 2018, less than two years after winning election to the Minnesota state legislature. Her decision to run was prompted by the surprise announcement that the incumbent, Democrat Keith Ellison, was vacating the seat to run for state Attorney General. It is important to note that Ellison was the first African-American to represent Minnesota in Congress and the first Muslim ever to serve in the House of Representatives. Ellison's announcement, coming just ten weeks before the Democratic primary led to a flurry of candidate filings and a fast-paced, condensed Democratic primary campaign.

Despite facing serious competition and multiple structural challenges, Omar won the primary decisively, with 48 percent of the vote (see Table 3.1) beating her closest Democratic opponent Margaret Anderson Kelliher by 16 percentage points. After securing the Democratic nomination, as well as the endorsement of the incumbent Keith Ellison, Omar was on a glide path to victory due to the strongly Democratic leanings of the district. The Republican candidate, Jennifer Zielinski, did not have political experience or meaningful support from the Republican party, raising less than $25,000 compared to Ilhan Omar's fundraising total of a little over one million (Federal Election Commission). Omar won the general election with 78 percent of the vote.

TABLE 3.1 Characteristics and Outcomes of Competitors for Minnesota's 5th Congressional District, Democratic Primary, and General Election, 2018

	Elected Office(s) held as of 2018	Age in years (August 2018)	Fundraising totals ($)[a]	Vote Totals[a]	Vote Percentage[a]
Democratic Primary—August 14, 2018					
Ilhan Omar	Minnesota House of Representatives, 2017–2018	36	481,492	65,237	48.2
Margaret Anderson Kelliher	Minnesota House of Representatives, 1999–2011★	50	535,860	41,156	30.4
Patricia Torres Ray	Minnesota State Senate, 2001–2013	54	96,971	17,629	13.0
Jamal Abdulahi	None	Unknown	148,773	4,984	3.7
Frank Drake	None	Unknown	N/A	2,460	1.8
General Election—November 6, 2018					
Ilhan Omar	Minnesota House of Representatives, 2017–2018	36	1,084,183	267,703	78.0
Jennifer Zielinski	None	Unknown	23,354.81	74.440	21.7

[a] Source: Federal Election Commission.

★ Speaker of MN House 2007–2011.

Given the heavily Democratic leanings of the district, Omar faced her only meaningful competition during the Democratic primary contest. The 5th Congressional District of Minnesota has a Cook Partisan Voter Index of +26, which means that recent Democratic presidential candidates performed on average 26 points better in this district than in the nation (see Table 3.2). This makes the 5th Congressional District the most Democratic district in the state of Minnesota as well as one of the most progressive in the country (Saleh 2018). While Omar's general election victory was predictable, there are several reasons why Omar's victory in the Democratic primary an against-the-odds success and a truly historic achievement.

The first challenge Omar faced concerned her relative lack of experience. Although Omar did not face an incumbent in the Democratic primary for the 5th Congressional District, as she did in her campaign for the state legislative seat, she still faced serious competition from experienced politicians. Omar, of course, was not a political amateur when she launched her congressional bid. Rather she was what Jacobson and Carson (2019) label a quality candidate, as she had state legislative experience under her belt. Serving in state legislatures has long been the most common path to power for members of Congress (Elder 2008; Maestas, Maisel, and Stone 2005). This holds true for the 116th Congress as well, in which 46 percent of the members have state legislative experience (Ramsdell 2019).

Yet, Omar's political experience did not distinguish her from her competitors. In fact, two of her competitors had significantly more political experience (Karnowski 2018). Margaret Kelliher had served for over two decades in the Minnesota House of Representatives holding multiple leadership roles including Speaker of the House and a lengthy list of impressive policy accomplishments (Saleh 2018). She also had experience running a state-wide election as the Democratic candidate for governor in 2010. Her considerable political experiences help explain her status as the fundraising leader during the primary phase of this race (see Table 3.1). Omar's other strongest challenge was Patricia Torres Ray, who had 12 years as a Minnesota State Senator under her belt as she launched her bid. For some within the Democratic establishment, Omar's relative lack of experience was a weakness (Saleh 2018).

There were two other candidates of note in the crowded primary field, but they arguably had less political experience than the others. One was Jamal Abdulahi, who like Omar is Somali American. While he had experience as a political activist and community organizer and held leadership positions in the Minnesota state Democratic Party, he had not previously held elected office. The other candidate was Frank Drake, who had run for this same congressional seat in 2016, but as a Republican challenging Keith Ellison in the general election. He too had never held elective office (Saleh 2018). Thus, most political observers viewed the 2018 Democratic primary as being mostly a competition between Margaret Kelliher, Ilhan Omar, and Patricia Torres Ray (Saleh 2018).

Omar's highly progressive positions and campaign themes appeared to resonate well with the liberal district she sought to represent, yet the reality is that her stances were not very different from the other Democratic candidates. All the major candidates were from the progressive wing of the party and all supported single payer health care, gun control, abolishing the Immigration and Customs Enforcement Agency, using the power of government more aggressively to fight climate change, and making college more affordable/ending the student debt crisis (Saleh 2018; Witt 2018).

On top of this Omar was a Black, immigrant, woman running for Congress in a country where sexism, racism, and anti-immigrant sentiment remain active currents within the American electorate. Moreover, Omar was vying to represent a majority white district, which was something very few Black women had been successful in doing (Lublin 2018). Most Black and Latino members of Congress represent majority-minority districts, congressional districts wherein many of the constituents are of color. Many of these districts were drawn in response to the 1965 Voting Rights Act and subsequent reauthorizations. While the 5th district of Minnesota is more diverse than the state overall (see Table 3.2), whites still form 62.8 percent of the district. Additionally, Omar was not the only woman of color in the race. Patricia Torres Ray shared Omar's status as a path-breaking woman of color, becoming the first Latina in the Minnesota Senate when she won her first election in 2006 (Saleh 2018). Thus, the race essentially came down to three

TABLE 3.2 Resident Characteristics of Minnesota's 5th Congressional District, Minnesota, and United States

	Minnesota 5th Congressional District[a]	Minnesota[b]	United States[b]
Average Age	33.7	38.2	28.2
Education			
Bachelors Degree or Higher (%)	47.8	36.7	32.6
Average Per Capita Income ($)	39,141	37,192	33,831
Percent in Poverty	14.0	9.6	13.1
Race/Ethnicity (%)			
White	62.8	79.5	60.4
Black	16.9	6.8	13.4
Latinx/Hispanic	9.5	5.5	18.3
Asian/Pacific Islander	5.9	5.2	6.1
Foreign Born	15.4	8.6	13.7
Persons who speak language other than English at home	21.7	12.2	21.9
Cook Political Report Partisan Index[c]	+26	+1	N/A

[a] Source: U.S. Census Bureau (2018). *American Community Survey 5-year estimates.* Retrieved from *Census Reporter Profile page for Congressional District 5, MN* http://censusreporter.org/profiles/50000US2705-congressional-district-5-mn/

[b] Source: Population Estimates, American Community Survey, Census of Population and Housing, Current Population Survey, Small Area Health Insurance Estimates, Small Area Income and Poverty Estimates, State and County Housing Unit Estimates, County Business Patterns, Non-employer Statistics, Economic Census, Survey of Business Owners, Building Permits. Retrieved from www.census.gov/quickfacts/fact/table/MN,US/RHI125218

Cook Political Report. https://cookpolitical.com/pvi-map-and-district-list

progressive women—one white, one Black, and one Latina—vying to represent a district that is 62.8 percent white, 16.9 percent Black, and 9.5 percent Latinx—an electoral environment in which most cases has typically favored the white candidate (Lublin 2018).

The keys to Omar's surprising success appear twofold. The first is that Ilhan Omar benefited from a significant amount of free media. Ilhan Omar's historic election to the Minnesota state legislature had resulted in a tremendous amount of positive media coverage at the local and national level, including being featured on the cover of *Time* magazine and in a Maroon 5 music video (Saleh 2018). In an original interview conducted by Stefanie Chambers, one of the co-authors of this chapter, a Somali American resident of the 5th Congressional District explained the power of Omar's media in this way:

> By the time she ran for Congress, she had received national—even international attention—as the first Somali American to serve in a state legislature

in the United States. She had tremendous name recognition and was seen as a new leader willing to give voice to groups without a place at the table. She was not just speaking for Somali Americans, but all Minnesotans who wanted a new leader to amplify their voices.

Community interview 11/27/2019

Of course, not all the media coverage Omar received in the lead up to the 2018 election was positive. As Ward (2016) has shown in her empirical analyses of congressional campaigns, women of color who run for Congress often face disproportionately negative media coverage. This was true in Omar's case. Omar had to confront negative news stories accusing her of marrying her brother and committing immigration fraud, claims raised by conservatives (Forliti 2018). Even though some of the media coverage was negative, the large amount of media attention devoted to Omar in the months following her election to the Minnesota state legislature translated into high name recognition, a traditionally valuable resource in congressional elections, which helped Omar gain traction over her more experienced competitors.

Second, original interview data with Americans living in the 5th Congressional District as well as newspaper accounts of the 2018 Democratic primary indicate that Omar's success was a product of her ability to draw on her multifaceted identities and lived experiences. Using her status as a young mother of three children, as an immigrant, as a Muslim who wears the hijab, as a Black woman, as a young professional with college debt, and as a renter in need of affordable housing, she was able to authentically connect with voters who saw themselves in her candidacy. Consequently, she assembled a diverse electoral coalition to support her candidacy.

This aspect of Omar's victory can be best understood through the theory of symbolic empowerment. In her book, *Historic Firsts: How Symbolic Empowerment Changes U.S. Politics* (2015), Evelyn Simien carefully analyzed the way a number of historic firsts—the Democratic presidential nomination quests of Shirley Chisholm in 1972, Jesse Jackson in 1984, and Hillary Clinton and Barack Obama in 2008—were able to mobilize unusually diverse coalition through the power of symbolic empowerment, the idea that marginalized groups can be inspired to political engagement and action by seeing someone who looks like them pursuing high level political office. For example, Simien finds that both Jesse Jackson in 1984 and Barack Obama in 2008 acted as mobilizing agents for African-American citizens as they pursued the Democratic presidential nomination. The African-American supporters of Jackson and Obama were not only more likely to vote in the nomination process, but more likely to engage in a range of political actions consistent with engaged citizenship.

In a similar way, Omar was able to achieve historic political victories by drawing on her intersecting identities and strong campaign skills to assemble a diverse coalition of voters. Throughout her campaign Omar argued that the historic nature of her candidacy and the fact that she embodied a perspective that was largely absent from Congress made her the candidate best positioned to understand and advocate for the issues affecting marginalized and underrepresented communities (Saleh 2018). The symbolic empowerment of Omar's candidacy can be seen through Omar's ability to attract and mobilize immigrant communities, Black Minnesotans, young progressives, women, and benefit from unusually high turnout.

As touched on previously, interviews, newspaper accounts and other data suggest that Omar drew on her experience as a first-generation immigrant living in "Trump's America" to effectively mobilize and gain the support of the immigrant community in her district. As Table 3.2 shows 15 percent of the Minnesota's 5th Congressional District is foreign born and 22 percent of people in the district speak a language other than English. The 5th district is in fact home to the largest Somali community in the United States and home to other immigrant groups including East Africans and Hmong. Table 3.3 includes an overview of the foreign-born population in the district. East Africans, Southeast Asians, and Latinos comprise the main immigrant communities.

It is important to note that Omar was not the only immigrant, nor was she the only Somali immigrant running in the Democratic primary. Nevertheless, Omar's candidacy and emphasis on the value of immigrants in American society seems to have resonated strongly within immigrant communities including the Somali community. Stefanie Chambers, one of the authors of this chapter, spent several years conducting interviews for her book *Somalis in the Twin Cities and Columbus: Immigrant Incorporation in New Destinations* (2017). During the time

TABLE 3.3 Region of Origin for Foreign-Born Residents of Minnesota's 5th Congressional District

Region of Origin	Total	Proportion (%)
Europe	9,342	8.7
Asia	28,949	26.8
Southeast Asia[a]	10,763	10.0
Africa	36,090	33.4
East Africa[b]	26,961	25.0
Americas	33,223	30.8
Oceania[c]	322	0.3
Total	107,926	100

Source: U.S. Census Bureau (2014–2018). Place of Birth for the Foreign-born Population in the United States American Community Survey 5-year estimates. Retrieved from https://censusreporter.org.

[a] Southeast Asia refers to Cambodia, Indonesia, Laos, Malaysia, Burma, Philippines, Singapore, Thailand, and Vietnam.
[b] East Africa refers to Eritrea, Ethiopia, Kenya, and Somalia.
[c] Oceania refers to Australia, New Zealand, and Fiji.

Chambers was interviewing Somali Americans in Minnesota, Ilhan Omar was a well-known city hall staffer and even then, Omar was a source of significant inspiration for the Somali community. In a 2018 op-ed in Minnesota's *Star Tribune* Chambers notes:

> During one interview with a group of Somali youth leaders, one woman told me: "She fights for what she believes in and has a public presence. We admire her willingness to stand up for the things she believes are right. She's smart and knows how the system works … She's our mentor."
>
> *Chambers 2018*

Omar's campaign spoke specifically to and about immigrants and their experience. Newspaper reports recount how Somali Americans and other immigrant groups living in Minnesota were highly inspired by Omar's campaign and entered conventional politics for the first time in their lives to work on her Democratic primary campaign and to vote in the Democratic primary (Fadel 2018; Herrera and Majerle 2018). One 25-year-old Somali American who voted for Omar in the August 14, 2018 Democratic primary stated that, "Before Ilhan, I think a lot of us didn't know what type of government we had, but now that she was elected, a lot of us started paying attention" (Farabaugh 2018). Similarly, the AP reported that Omar's victory in the 2018 Democratic primary "depended heavily on support from people who feel persecuted in Trump's America and voters who empathize with them" (Karnowski 2018).

Another key part of Omar's electoral coalition were young progressives. The 5th Congressional District of Minnesota represents a swatch of the University of Minnesota and thus is unusually young, with a median age 34, making it one of the youngest districts in the United States. By being the youngest of the candidates (see Table 3.1) while also emphasizing experiences common among young Americans—such as her status as a renter and a young professional with college debt—Omar was also able to connect with and mobilize young voters, a group with notoriously low turnout. While all the major candidates were from the progressive wing of the party, Omar was able to secure key endorsements from progressive groups including MoveOn and the Our Revolution, which emerged out of Bernie Sanders' 2016 presidential bid, a campaign with high levels of popularity among young Americans (Saleh 2018). Inspiring unusually high turnout among college students was a key aspect of Omar's 2016 victory for the state legislature and this was repeated, once again, in the 2018 congressional primary.

While women of color face a double bind in many respects due to racism and sexism, scholars such as Katherine Tate (1997) and Wendy Smooth (2018) have argued that key to the electoral victories of women of color, especially Black women as congressional candidates, has been their ability to draw on pre-existing networks and resources from both the Black community and the network or groups devoted to supporting women's candidacies. This appears to have been a key feature in Omar's victory as well. After being elected to the overwhelmingly white Minnesota state legislature (95 percent white), Omar worked hard to connect with and represent the concerns of people of color in her district and address the dramatic inequalities by race in Minnesota directly (Witt 2018). Omar helped to create the Minnesota House People of Color and Indigenous caucus (Saleh 2018) and received key endorsements from one of the co-founders of Black Lives Matter (Witt 2018). Additionally, Women Winning, which has been described as a PAC that "is essentially the local equivalent of EMILY's List" gave their endorsement to Omar (Saleh 2018), even though her top competitors were other experienced progressive women. This endorsement not only provided Omar's campaign with resources but acted as an important signal to progressive women interested in electing a woman that Omar was their best choice. This is particularly important given that the voters in the Democratic primary tend to be disproportionately women.

Contextualizing Representative Omar's Congressional Victory and Leadership

Ilhan Omar's election to Congress also should be understood within the broader context of the intersection of women's representation and partisan polarization in the United States. Partisan polarization has come to shape every facet of American political life, including the representation of women in elective office. As the Democratic and Republican parties diverged ideologically with the Democrats becoming a more progressive party and Republicans moving significantly to the right, representation of women among Republicans in Congress has gone down, while Democratic women have made steady and impressive gains (Elder 2020). Partisan realignment over issues of race, and the Democratic party's evolution over the 20th century to become the party of civil rights, racial equality, and inclusivity (Carmines and Stimson 1989) has resulted in exceptionally high levels of Democratic partisanship among voters as well as legislators of color at both the state and national level (Tate 1994). President Trump's 2016 campaign and governing style, which integrates appeals to racial and ethnic resentment as well as anti-immigrant sentiments have further polarized the parties over issues of race, ethnicity, and immigration (Abramowitz and McCoy 2019; Hooghe and Dassoneville 2018; Jardina 2019). As a result of the partisan realignment over issues of race, almost all of women of color in Congress are Democrats.

It is in this political context that the 2018 election, and the victory of Ilhan Omar, took place. The 2018 elections were historic for women with the biggest jump ever in terms of the number of women elected to Congress. Yet, these gains were exclusively among Democrats. Ilhan Omar was part of this historic wave of Democratic women candidates. As of 2019, women comprise 38 percent of Democrats in the U.S. House and are on a steady track to reach proportionate representation in the Democratic Party caucus. In contrast, the number of Republican women in the House dropped from 23 to 13 in the wake of the 2018 election. Women form only six percent of House Republicans, a smaller share than they did several decades ago (Elder 2020). As a result of these divergent trends, the 116th Congress (2019–2021) is characterized by a historically large partisan gap among its women members, with Democrats comprising 83 percent of women in the House (Elder 2021).

The wave of freshman women lawmakers elected in 2018 are also historic-ally diverse. There are now a record number of Black, Latinx, Native American, and Asian American women in Congress (Dittmar 2019). With the retirement of Republican Representative Ileana Ros-Lehtinen and the loss of Republican Mia Love in 2018, every woman of color serving in the 116th Congress, except one, is a Democrat.

Ilhan Omar is also part of a "new wave" of Black members of Congress who are representing majority-white districts. As mentioned previously, most people of color serving in Congress represent majority minority districts. Yet in 2018, eight new Black Americans were elected to Congress in majority-white districts (Lublin 2018). Half of this group were women, and one of them was Omar. In contrast to prior generations of Black candidates seeking to represent majority white districts or states, who pursued deracialized campaigns and governing styles (Sonenshein 1990), Ilhan Omar embraced her multi-faceted identity as an asset in her campaign.

There are three main takeaways from this contextual review. The first is that the Democratic Party's return to majority status in the U.S. House of Representatives in the wake of the 2018 election and future hold on power is meaningfully dependent on the strong performance of women candidates of color, such as Ilhan Omar and the other historic first women covered in this volume. Second, Omar's potential political power, and the influence of women of color in Congress more broadly, is very much tied to the fate of the Democratic Party and more specific-ally rooted within the progressive wing of the Democratic Party. Third and related, this increasingly diverse Democratic caucus is now facing a Republican Party caucus in Congress that has become even more dominated by white men, and that is increasingly drawing on anti-immigrant sentiments and racial resentment to win elections (Hetherington, Long and Rudolph 2016).

Congresswoman Omar in Trump's America

Any discussion of the political experience of Ilhan Omar would be incomplete without contextualizing her rise during the Trump administration. In many ways, her campaign and election to Congress stand in stark contrast to the leadership of President Trump, a leader who frequently makes anti-immigrant pronouncements and played a key role in limiting refugee resettlement in the United States. In fact, during a 2016 campaign stop in Minnesota, Trump voiced his concerns about Somalis in Minnesota. He stated: "Here in Minnesota, you have seen firsthand the problems caused with faulty refugee vetting, with large numbers of Somali refugees coming into your state, without your knowledge, without your support or approval (Lee 2016)."

There are several problems with Trump's pronouncement, including the fact that Minnesota has a long history of refugee resettlement and that the careful vetting process used by the U.S. government resulted in a highly effective and careful screening process (Chambers 2017). It was in the context of these and other derogatory comments from candidate and President Trump that Ilhan Omar officially entered the national stage. Once elected, Trump specifically targeted Omar and other members of "the squad." In one particularly shocking moment in July 2019 he said that they should all "go back" to where they came from (Rogers and Fandos 2019). Further, he stated: "Why don't they go back and help fix the totally broken and crime infested places from which they came. Then come back and show us how it is done" (in Rogers and Fandos 2019).

Of course, it is ironic that Representative Omar is the only member of the squad not born in the United States. More importantly, Trump's comments serve as a dog whistle to his base, many of whom see women of color in Congress as a threat to the nation. As jarring as some of Trump's comments have been, Omar has continued to fight back, calling him a "fascist" and stating "We are going to continue to be a nightmare to this president because his policies are a nightmare to us. We are not deterred. We are not frightened" (Fram and Superville 2019).

In some ways, Trump's attacks have raised national awareness of Omar and increased her influence. According to some respondents, Trump's attacks have also boosted Omar's fundraising (Community interview 10/31/2019; Community interview 11/27/2019). At the same time, it's impossible not to acknowledge the obstacles created by Trump's vitriolic rhetoric. Omar has received numerous death threats and her family has been forced to take extreme safety measures (Community interview 11/27/2019). But she also made several statements that were criticized for being anti-Semitic since her election to Congress (Rahman 2019). In fact, some of her comments about the power of the Jewish lobby in the United States have been criticized by her fellow Democrats and prompted House Democrats to bring a resolution to the House floor condemning anti-Semitism and Islamophobia (Shabad et al. 2019). Trump also tweeted a video of comments she made in March 2018 about how the civil rights of Muslim Americans were violated after 9/11 terror attacks. This tweet positioned her comments against an image of the Twin Towers ablaze, prompting outrage by fellow Democrats. Defenders of Omar claim that she supports Jews but takes issue with the United States' positions on the Israeli-Palestinian conflict. Conservative media outlets have amplified her controversial comments and increased the negative attention she receives. Objectively, her comments have brought her into one of the taboo areas of American foreign policy. Whether this is due to her commitment to Palestinian rights or political missteps by a relative novice, she continues to have to defend her claims that she is not an anti-Semite.

U.S. Representative Ilhan Omar and Symbolic Empowerment

Since winning election to Congress, Ilhan Omar has continued to empower historically unrepresented and marginalized communities. Much of our evidence about the symbolically empowering effect of Omar's presence on the national stage comes from in-depth interviews with Somali Americans in Minnesota. Interviews with members of the Somali American community offer support for the idea that Omar's candidacy and election to Congress made them think differently about elected politics. During a 2019 interview, one Somali American respondent coined the term the "Ilhan Effect" to describe the symbolically empowering impact of Ilhan Omar's rise. He explained:

> In the Muslim community, the Ilhan effect is the most pronounced. From the outside people see this Muslim woman, a Somali, and it's a novelty. But it's much bigger effect within the community. There have been people involved in the DFL for years and they never would have considered running for office, but now they see that if she can do it, so can they! There are all these races where Muslims are now running for office, at the state level and for Congress. I don't think they would be doing it if Ilhan had not won. If someone in front of you breaks a barrier, it's more likely that someone will follow.
>
> *Community interview 10/31/2019*

This assessment resonated with how other respondents viewed her victory and symbolic influence. Another respondent specifically focused his comments on the impact of Omar's leadership on youth. He explained:

> Her biggest impact is our young girls. I have two young daughters. Last week my daughter watched the documentary "Time for Ilhan" at her internship. She called me and said "I want to be like Ilhan! This is amazing and I'm inspired!" And I've heard this throughout our community from young girls and boys too. So, her impact is amazingly touching lives. Her victories have told young girls who experience racism, Islamophobia, sexism, and those sorts of things in school that they can be like Ilhan. A voice for equality. Her message has reached a lot of kids. They think they can shoot for the moon. Whether it's education, organizing, running for office. So, the biggest issue now is that we have so many young people who are empowered.
>
> *Community interview 8/12/2019 a*

Another respondent with firsthand experience with Omar's early political aspirations said:

She is humble and generous with others. She sees that she is just one person and that there is room for many more at the table. Her dedication to helping others coming up behind her is really an important part of her story.

Community interview 11/27/2019

Finally, one respondent specifically noted how Congresswoman Omar is giving voice to immigrants and refugees at a time when these vulnerable groups are most in need of support. His comments also reference the idea that through Omar, a vulnerable community that is often misrepresented has a chance for more accurate representation. This respondent said:

As we know, in the American Context of diversity, we say that it's one nation under God and we're all equal. But at the same time, we also know that people need somebody to speak for them, elected officials. So, Somalis especially are going through a tough time because they are a new wave of immigrants. Somalia is a country that has had some very difficult situations. To have someone in Congress who can point to the needs of refugees in general, and the role of immigrants who came as refugees and their successes is important. The fact that she is a refugee who ascended to Congress is a really powerful story. So, I think that will bring to light many of the false accusations that are brought against the community.

Community interview 8/12/2019

Given Ilhan Omar's highly visible national profile, it is likely she has served as a symbol of empowerment not just for Somali Americans within her district, but outside of her district and outside of Minnesota. Moreover, her explicitly inter-sectional identity—as a Black woman, a Somali refugee, and a Muslim—suggests that she may be offering symbolic representation to a range of underrepresented and marginalized groups in American politics. Uhlaner and Scola (2016) have demonstrated that symbolic representation and minority empowerment extends beyond legislative boundaries and that the presence of minority candidates and legislators increases turnout.

Ilhan Omar appears to have inspired and provided symbolic leadership to other young women, Somalis, and Muslims to run for office. Young Somali women who ran for local office in 2018 credited Ilhan Omar with inspiring them to run for local government offices (Herrera and Majerle 2018). And in 2019, a record number of Somali Americans and Muslim Americans ran for state and local level offices across the country (Council on American-Islamic Relations 2019). Ghazala Hashmi, for example, defeated a Republican incumbent to win elected to the Virginia state legislature, the first Muslim American woman ever to do so (Haltiwanger 2019). The 2019 election also resulted in the election of a 23-year-old Somali American Democrat, Nadia Mohamed, to the city council in St. Louis Park, Minnesota (Haltiwanger 2019). Another 23-year-old Democrat and Somali American named

Safiya Khalid won a seat on Lewiston, Maine's city council (Haltiwanger 2019). And finally, Abrar Omeish, another Muslim and female Democrat, was elected to an at-large school board position in Fairfax County, Virginia (Haltiwanger 2019). While it's too early to tell whether this trend of Somali and Muslim women running and winning positions in elective office will continue, many credit Ilhan Omar with inspiring their decision to run (Community interview 11/27/2019).

Conclusion

Ilhan Omar's presence in American politics is historic in many ways. She is the first Somali American to serve in Congress. She is also one of the first two Muslim women to serve in this institution. Finally, she is currently the only former refugee serving in Congress. Yet, beyond these distinctive firsts, it is perhaps the intersection of all these identities and Omar's embrace of these identities in her campaigns and as a representative in Congress that make Omar such a path-breaking figure in American politics.

Like historic firsts who came before her, interviews and newspaper accounts suggest that Ilhan Omar's political ascendance was due in part to the ways she motivated historically marginalized and underrepresented groups to become politically engaged to volunteer for her campaign, and to turn out to vote in higher numbers than usual. Her political ascendance also highlights the importance of nurturing political ambition in women at a young age. Because he needed her to be his translator, Omar's grandfather immersed her in Democratic Party politics in Minnesota when she was a young teen and these experiences of attending party meetings and seeing people advocate for their positions inspired her to want to make a difference through public service (Witt 2018). Interviews with the Somali American community suggest Omar's election to Congress may be continuing to inspire a new generation of young women and that those who share aspects of her life story might be empowered to follow in her footsteps and run for political office someday.

An important element of Omar's political ascendance is that she did not "wait her turn" or wait to be asked to throw her hat in the ring. Omar's first step into elective office came not because of recruitment by the Democratic Party or biding her time until there was a vacancy, but rather because of running against an established incumbent within her own party. Ilhan Omar won her first elected position in the Minnesota state house by taking on and vanquishing a well-established incumbent in her own party. This is like the route of another historic firsts highlighted in this volume, Ayanna Pressley (D-MA), who came to power by challenging a long-serving incumbent in the Democratic party (Dittmar 2019).

Finally, Omar's rise to power and potential influence must be understood through the lens of partisanship and party power. Omar is now one of the 43 women of color serving in Congress. All these women except one are Democrats. In terms of the image young people see when they look at Congress it is a stark divide: they see a diverse Democratic Party, where women form close to 40 percent of Democrats in Congress and women color are well-represented, versus a Republican Party where women form less than 10 percent of the caucus and there is only one women of color. It is important to note that Ilhan Omar and the other members of The Squad all won re-election in their 2020 Democratic primaries and are all but certain to be returned to Congress in January 2021. Ilhan Omar along with Rashida Tlaib were able to defeat well-funded challengers in their primary races. Their 2020 victories suggest that rather than their elections being an anomaly of the 2018 midterms, these progressive, young, diverse women are on track to become a critical component of the future of the Democratic Party. While these women are changing the face and policies of the Democratic Party, it is also the case that the power of Omar and the other historic firsts featured in this volume is intimately tied to the fate of the Democratic Party. Their ability to influence policy beyond symbolic representation is in many ways tied to both the congressional and presidential outcomes of 2020.

Notes

1 Using Nexis Uni, 1,038 articles from the *Star Tribune* were reviewed from January 2014–January 2020.
2 In Minnesota, the Democratic Party is known as the Democratic Farm Labor Party, or DFL. This is a progressive wing of the Democratic Party. For simplicity, we refer to the DFL as the Democratic Party because all of Minnesota's DFL representatives caucus with the Democrats at the national level.

References

Abramowitz, Alan, and Jennifer McCoy. 2019. "United States: Racial Resentment, Negative Partisanship, and Polarization in Trump's America." *The Annals of the American Academy of Political and Social Science* 681(1): 137–156.

Bierschback, Briana, and Ibrahhim, Hirsi. 2016. "Ilhan Omar Defeats Longtime Rep. Phyllis Khan in Historic Primary Win." Minnpost, August 10, 2016.

Brewer, Sierra, and Lauren Dundes. 2018. "Concerned, meet Terrified: Intersectional Feminism and the Women's March." *Women's Studies International Forum*, 69(July–August): 49–55.

Carmines, Edward G., and James S. Stimson. 1989. *Issue Evolution: Race and the Transformation of American Politics*. Princeton, NJ: Princeton University Press.

Cook Political Report. 2020. Partisan Voter Index (PVI) https://cookpolitical.com/pvi-map-and-district-list.

Council on American-Islamic Relations. 2019. *The Rise of American Muslim Changemakers: Political Organizing in the Trump Era*. www.jstor.org/stable/resrep31107.11. Chambers, Stefanie. 2017. *Somalis in the Twin Cities and Columbus: Immigrant Incorporation in New Destinations*. Philadelphia, PA: Temple University Press.

Chambers, Stefanie. 2018. "In winning U.S. House primary, Ilhan Omar breaks barriers and sets an Example." *Star Tribune,* August 16, 2018.

Community interview 4/14/2020.

Community interview 11/27/2019.

Community interview 10/31/2019.

Community interview 8/12/2019.

Community interview 8/12/ 2019 a.

Congressional Research Service. 2019. Membership of the 116th Congress: A Profile. https://crsreports.congress.gov/product/pdf/R/R45583.

Darcy, R., Janet Clark, and Susan Welch. 1994. *Women, Elections and Representation*. 2nd ed. Lincoln, Nebraska: University of Nebraska Press.

Dittmar, Kelly. 2019. *Unfinished Business: Women Running in 2018 and Beyond*. Center for American Women and Politics (CAWP), Eagleton Institute of Politics, New Brunswick, NJ.

Elder, Laurel. 2008. "Whither Republican Women: The Growing Partisan Gap among Women in Congress." *The Forum* 6(1): Article 13. www.bepress.com/forum/vol6/iss1/art13.

Elder, Laurel. 2020. "The Growing Partisan Gap among Women in Congress." *Society* 57: 520–526. https://doi.org/10.1007/s12115-020-00524-0.

Elder, Laurel. 2021. *The Partisan Gap: Why Democratic Women Get Elected, But Republican Women Don't*. New York University Press.

Fadel, Leila. 2018. "Muslims Hope to 'Wake Up' At the Ballot Box This Year. *NPR, Morning Edition,* November 5.

Farabaugh, Kane. 2018. "Ilhan Omar Close to Becoming First African Refugee in US Congress." *Voices of America,* August 15.

Forliti, Amy. 2018. "Minnesota House hopeful calls marriage, fraud claims lies." *Associated Press*, October 17, 2018.

Fram, Alan, and Darlene Superville. 2019. "Rep. Ilhan Omar Vows to be 'Nightmare' for Trump." *Washington Times,* July 18, 2019.

Geiger, Abigail. 2019. "In 116th Congress, at least 13% of lawmakers are immigrants of the children of immigrants." *Pew Research Center*, January 24. www.immigrationresearch.org/node/2640.

Haltiwanger, John. 2019. "Muslim Women and Refugees Won Historic Victories across the US in Tuesday's Elections." *Business Insider,* November 6, 2019. www.businessinsider.com/muslim-women-refugees-won-historic-victories-in-tuesday-elections-2019-11.

Herrera, Allison, and Peter Majerle. 2018. "'In Love with Democracy,' Ilhan Omar Draws Diverse Supporters in Her Bid for Congress." *Pittsburgh Post-Gazette,* November 4, 2018.

Hetherington, Mark J., Meri T. Long, Thomas J. Rudolph. 2016. "Revisiting the Myth: New Evidence of a Polarized Electorate." *Public Opinion Quarterly* 80(1): 321–350.

Hooghe, Marc, and Ruth Dassonneville. 2018. "Explaining the Trump Vote: The Effect of Racist Resentment and Anti-Immigrant Sentiments." *Political Science & Politics* 51(3): 528–534.

Jacobson, Gary, and Jamie L. Carson. 2019. *The Politics of Congressional Elections*. Lanhan, MD: Rowman and Littlefield.

Jardina, Ashley. 2019. "White Consciousness and White Prejudice: Two Compounding Forces in Contemporary American Politics." *The Forum* 17(3): 447–466. Retrieved November 13, 2019, from doi:10.1515/for-2019-0025.

Karnowski, Steve. 2018 "Victory offers Muslim Candidate New Platform to Oppose Trump." *Associated Press,* August 15, 2018.

Lee, Esther Yu His. 2016. "Trump Equates Somali Refugees in Minnesota to Terrorists." *Think Progress*, November 7, 2016. https://thinkprogress.org/trump-somali-immigrants-refugees-minnesota-c376bdec76f4/.

Lublin, David. 2018. "Eight white majority Districts elected Black Members of Congress this Year: That's a Breakthrough." *The Washington Post*, November 9, 2018.

Maestas, Cherie D., L. Sandy Maisel, and Walter J. Stone. 2005. "National Party Efforts to Recruit State Legislators to Run for the U.S. House." *Legislative Studies Quarterly* 30(2): 277–300.

Ramsdell, Molly. 2019. "Former State Legislators in the 116th Congress." *National Conference of State Legislatures* [blog], January 14.

Rahman, Khaleda. 2019. "Ilhan Omar Faces Fresh Accusations of Anti-Semitism Over Michael Bloomberg Tweet." *Newsweek,* November 10, 2019.

Rogers, Katie, and Nicholas Fandos. "Trump Tells Congresswoman to 'Go Back' to the Countries They Came From." *The New York Times*, July 14, 2019.

Saleh, Maryam. 2018. "There's 'No Question' A Progressive Woman Will Replace Keith Ellison in Congress. But Who Will It Be?" *The Intercept*, August 10.

Simien, Evelyn. 2015. *Historic Firsts: How Symbolic Empowerment Changes US politics*. New York: Oxford University Press.

Smooth, Wendy. 2018. "African American Women and Electoral Politics: The Core of the New American Electorate." In *Gender & Elections: Shaping the Future of American Politics, fourth edition*, eds. Susan J. Carroll and Richard L. Fox. New York, NY: Cambridge University Press, 171–197.

Sonenshein, Raphael. J. 1990. "Can Black Candidates Win Statewide Elections?" *Political Science Quarterly* 105(2): 219–241.

Tate, Katherine. 1994. *From Protest to Politics: The New Black Voters in American Elections, enlarged edition*. Cambridge, MA: Harvard University Press and the Russell Sage Foundation.

Tate, Katherine. 1997. "African American Female Senatorial Candidates: Twin Assets or Double Liabilities?" In *African American Power and Politics*, ed. Hanes Walton, Jr. New York, NY: Columbia University Press, pp. 264–281.

Uhlaner, Carole Jean, and Becki Scola. 2016. "Collective Representation as a Mobilizer: Race/Ethnicity, Gender, and their Intersections at the State Level." *State Politics & Policy Quarterly* 16(2): 227–263.

Ward, Orlanda. 2016. "Seeing Double: Race, Gender, and Coverage of Minority Women's Campaigns for the U.S. House of Representatives." *Politics and Gender* 12(2): 317–343.

Witt, Emily. 2018. "How Ilhan Omar Won Hearts in Minnesota's Fifth." *The New Yorker,* August 15.

Wong, Janelle S. 2019. "Race, Evangelicals, and Immigration." *The Forum* 17(3): 403–419.

4

AYANNA PRESSLEY

Change Can't Wait

Lauren E. Jones and Evelyn M. Simien

Boston City Councilor Ayanna Pressley was elected to serve the Massachusetts 7th Congressional District on November 6, 2018, becoming the first Black woman from Massachusetts elected to the U.S. Congress and the first person of color to represent its only majority-minority congressional district (which includes three quarters of Boston, and most of Cambridge). Pressley's election was a historic first, breaking a glass ceiling for women generally and shattering a concrete one for women of color. While Pressley was no political newcomer to the city of Boston, her campaign garnered widespread media attention on account of her victory— that is, having defeated a ten-term incumbent, Michael Capuano, of the same political party. Given similar policy views made it difficult to differentiate the two candidates, and incumbency remains a powerful barrier to increasing the number of women in Congressional office, such a racially and ethnically diverse district made descriptive and symbolic representation more relevant for the local voting eligible population.

By focusing on identity, making gender and race salient considerations, Pressley increased the likelihood that such categories of difference would become important references for electoral judgments. Pressley like Capuano could claim that in addition to exemplary public service on issues that disproportionately affect women and racial minorities—abortion and gun control—she offered an alternative public image of political leadership when the default category had been that of a white, heterosexual male for the last 20 years. That is to suggest context mattered, given the historic nature of the campaign and its mobilizing effect on the racially and ethnically diverse voting eligible population in the district. Pressley's own perception of her constituency and the votes she'd likely secure offered her a strategic advantage and determined her ground game as one that was linguistically and socially adept in multiple cultures. Pressley faced an American

DOI: 10.4324/9781003213925-4

electorate that was especially appreciative of what it perceived to be her unique authenticity and emotional intelligence derived from formative life experiences, dating back to childhood and early adulthood.

Unlike her opponent, she demonstrated the need for a "preferable descriptive representative" like herself—for example, she could speak on behalf of sexual assault survivors and children of incarcerated parents or parents suffering from a substance abuse disorder (Dovi 2002). Pressley was 19 when she was raped on the campus of Boston University, but prior to that she had endured years of childhood sexual abuse (Levenson and Ebbert 2018). Her father's struggle with a heroin addiction and his incarceration for 16 years intermittently placed her in a unique position to understand certain policy implications for the school to prison pipeline, community policing, and child welfare. These personal challenges made her relatable to constituents, connecting lived experience, political representation, and legislative issues to race, gender, and, in some cases, age. Thus, Pressley's personal narrative cannot be treated as an isolated biography when it provides guidance for understanding how the political context and demographic makeup of Boston shaped the impact of such an intersectional actor. Once she emerged onto the political scene as a historic first candidate, Pressley had to prioritize her policy preferences while holding party identification constant and reconciling the limits of her presence opposite an opponent with more seniority and an incumbency advantage with her call for descriptive and symbolic representation.

Given the American voters' interest in such domestic policy issues—substance abuse disorders, mass incarceration, and sexual assault—Pressley could establish a strong mutual relationship with dispossessed subgroup members of her home district, revitalize democracy and strengthen its legitimacy by moving beyond party and ideology to highlight differences between her and her opponent, Capuano, with a key contextual factor being the demographic makeup of the district. Holding true to her policy preferences, she was able to complicate what was thought to be their "limited policy differences" as both progressive members of the same political party by focusing on the salience of her multiple group identity as a woman of color. Her cumulative life experiences differed remarkably from her opponent, and more closely resembled that of local constituents. From a policy perspective, she stood to give prominence to issues that otherwise would have either been overlooked or ignored by a progressive white, male incumbent with the same party affiliation. Such identity markers as age, race, and gender alongside lived experience mattered insofar as they informed her policy perspective, and signaled differences between her and the incumbent. On this basis, Pressley could build trust in American governmental institutions and win election.

But is that all that led to a successful campaign? Our short answer is no. Few would argue that race and gender were the sole factors that determined Pressley's victory, given there is merit in identity—that is, in terms of the experience and perspective she would bring as a Black woman to the office and exercise of political leadership. Still, there were several other influential factors that interacted and functioned simultaneously that influenced the outcome of this election in 2018. To be sure, there is more to Ayanna Pressley's game-changing performance as a historic first. Analyzing this candidate centered campaign through an intersectional lens ensures a more complete picture of the myriad of dynamics and electioneering at play, including but not limited to, identity-based appeals and a meld of mobilization with coalition-building. Looking critically and with complexity at the role of race and gender in the electoral process is necessary to explore alternative ways of thinking about strategy for candidates, voters, and campaigns in cities like Boston and Cambridge that have become increasingly more diverse.

So, who is Ayanna Pressley? How did she achieve such a historic victory? Like her campaign strategy since becoming a Boston city councilor in 2009, Pressley forged a multiracial grassroots coalition that should remind readers of Shirley Chisholm's historic first candidacies—specifically, her becoming the first Black woman elected to the U.S. Congress in 1968 from New York. Chisholm brought formerly inactive people (those who previously saw no connection between campaigns and their own lives) into the electoral process. She established a strong mutual relationship with dispossessed subgroups from historically disadvantaged populations located within her district, as did Pressley, who similarly reached vulnerable populations who had been unjustly excluded from and stigmatized by the political process. She, like Chisholm, understood the process by which elected representatives "stood for" their constituents. Growing up, Ayanna witnessed the leadership of U.S. Congresswoman Shirley Chisholm and felt inspired by her commitment to fighting injustice while lifting the voices of historically marginalized Americans. Little did Pressley know that years later she, too, would successfully become a congresswoman and, in fact, work from the same office once occupied by Chisholm (Ruiz-Grossman 2018).

In this chapter, we start with an overview of Pressley's childhood and early adulthood. Then, we segue into an analysis of state and local politics in Boston, including the historical context and political landscape leading up to Pressley's bid for the U.S. House of Representatives. An introduction to Pressley's opponent, Congressman Michael Capuano, is provided and especially important when considering the complexities of her campaign. We cover Pressley's ground game, demonstrating how she strategically connected with voters and secured her primary win on September 4, 2018. This chapter is informed by a rich array of sources from campaign literature and newspaper accounts to public opinion and census data as well as interviews.

Destined to Be a Leader

Ayanna Pressley was born in Cincinnati, Ohio in 1974. She was raised in Chicago, Illinois by her mother, Sandy Pressley. As a single mother and tenant rights organizer, Sandy lived paycheck to paycheck (Levenson and Ebbert 2018). At an early age, Ayanna's mother exposed her to community organizing. Her mother also taught Ayanna to use her voice, and to be unapologetic when standing up for issues that mattered to her and their local community. Pressley's ambition was fueled by her religious upbringing, socioeconomic background, community activism, and local politics, as well as historic events. She accompanied her mother to tenant rights meetings, protests, marches, and political rallies, which cultivated a relationship with local government. At 10 years old, Ayanna joined her mother at the victory celebration of Harold Washington who was elected mayor of Chicago. He became the city's first Black mayor in the early 1980's (Levenson and Ebbert 2018). Despite numerous challenges during her youth, Pressley thrived at an exceptional college prep private school—the Francis W. Parker School—located in Chicago. She was president of student government, a cheerleader, a competitive debater, and voted "Most Likely to Become Mayor" of Chicago. Pressley was also the commencement speaker in her senior year (Levenson and Ebbert 2018).

Upon graduation, Pressley moved to Massachusetts to attend Boston University and her mother moved to New York City (Levenson and Ebbert 2018). As a freshman, Pressley served as student president of her college within the university (Levenson and Ebbert 2018). Pressley also organized a student event to honor Reverend Dr. Martin Luther King Jr.'s birthday and invited then U.S. Representative Joe Kennedy II as a guest speaker (Levenson and Ebbert 2018). Per this introduction, Pressley pursued an internship in the office of Congressman Joe Kennedy as a freshman (Levenson and Ebbert 2018). Despite a successful first year at Boston University, Pressley's college experience was quickly disrupted when she was raped on campus by someone she knew while working as a resident assistant the summer between her freshman and sophomore year (Levenson and Ebbert 2018). At the time, she felt too ashamed to report the incident; however, Pressley began sharing her story publicly years later (Levenson and Ebbert 2018). In her sophomore year, college came to a halt when Pressley's mother lost her job in New York City (Levenson and Ebbert 2018). To help support her mother, Pressley withdrew from college and worked full-time (Levenson and Ebbert 2018).

Once hired as a volunteer coordinator for then U.S. Senator John Kerry's 1996 re-election campaign against Massachusetts Governor William Weld, Pressley found herself weighing in on team decisions within a year and after Kerry's re-election, she landed a full-time job as a scheduler in his Washington, D.C. office. After 13 years of working in a variety of roles, including Constituent Services Director and Political Director, for U.S. Senator John Kerry of Massachusetts, Pressley returned to Boston to launch her first city councilor at-large campaign. Despite her experience working in politics, it was not typical in 2009 to have a native from Chicago, let alone an outspoken woman of color, jump into a political race in Boston. That said, it is important that we discuss the demographics of this major metropolitan city and its political history along with other historic first candidates as having paved the way and set the stage for Pressley's inaugural campaign and re-election campaigns as city councilor.

History and Political Landscape of Boston, Massachusetts

Boston represents the capital of Massachusetts, and the economic engine of the state. While Boston is among the most diverse cities in the country, many of its neighborhoods remain segregated by race and ethnicity (Schuster and Ciurczak 2018). The Hispanic/Latino population in the East Boston neighborhood accounts for 58 percent of the population compared to only 19 percent citywide; the Black/African-American population in Dorchester makes up 44 percent of the neighborhood's population yet 23 percent citywide; and 76 percent of Back Bay residents are non-Hispanic/white, much greater than the 45 percent share of non-Hispanic/white residents citywide.[1] Most Black residents live in such predominately Black neighborhoods as Hyde Park, Mattapan, Roxbury, and parts of Dorchester (Austin 2018, 40). They, who are non-immigrant and African-American, are the most marginalized both economically and politically of all minority groups in Boston. The median net worth for a white household in Greater Boston is $247,500 and yet the median net worth of a non-immigrant African-American household is only $8 (Muñoz et al. 2015).

Why is this? One root cause goes back to the era of school desegregation. While the desegregation of public schools became a nationally charged issue following the U.S. Supreme Court's 1954 ruling of *Brown v. Board of Education*, it took 20-plus years for Boston public schools to desegregate and only after a court order mandate issued by U.S. District Judge W. Arthur Garrity (Irons, Murphy, and Russell 2014). Following this ruling and its implementation, racial protests and riots ensued across Boston (Irons, Murphy, and Russell 2014). Over the next decade, it took more than 400 court orders to implement the city's busing plan between mainly Black and white neighborhoods (Irons, Murphy, and Russell 2014). During this transformational period for Boston and the Boston public schools, white student enrollment declined significantly. Today, minority populations represent 76 percent of the Boston public school student body (BPS Communications Office). During the era of school desegregation, other areas of local policy underwent change. In 1975, the city's at-large system for political representation was challenged by a group of African-American plaintiffs. They filed a federal class-action lawsuit claiming the at-large voting system prevented black candidates from winning seats on the city council and the five-member school board (Austin 2018). Even though the U.S. District Court determined the at-large system was legal, voters approved a city referendum to replace the at-large system (Austin 2018). As a result, a new city council in Boston was designed to include the seven-district plus four at-large, elected offices, rather than nine at-large offices (Austin 2018).

By the turn of the 21st century, political leadership remained sparse among Black state legislators, and entirely absent among Massachusetts constitutional offices and local elected offices in Boston. Yet, there was a rise of Black political newcomers, hailing from the Boston area. Marie St. Fleur and Linda Dorcena Forry—two Haitian women—were elected to the Massachusetts State House of Representatives from districts that included Dorchester, Mattapan, and Roxbury (Austin 2018). In 2006, Governor Deval L. Patrick, a business leader turned elected official from Milton—a town adjacent to Boston—became the state's first Black governor and the nation's second.

By 2009, Ayanna Pressley returned to Boston after working as an aide for U.S. Senator John Kerry in Washington, DC, and launched her first campaign for office. Pressley kicked off her campaign by raising awareness of issues that resonated with her personally including women's health and criminal justice reform; however, she was advised not to focus on such issues that would pigeon-hold the campaign and cost her votes. Pressley disregarded this advice, sharing her lived experience and vision for the city. She saw firsthand a city still scarred by the era of busing and desegregation. Her personal life story was all too familiar and resonated with residents who similarly had experienced trauma that did not discriminate by race, gender, or socioeconomic status across generations. She emerged as a relatable, public figure with whom voters could engage and feel good about, stoking their desire to get involved in the electoral process. Pressley implemented a "100 Club" campaign strategy, asking her supporters to recruit ten more registered voters to cast a ballot in her favor (Austin 2018). She also gained endorsements from women advocacy groups—namely, the Massachusetts Women's Political Caucus and the University of Massachusetts-Boston's Center for Women in Politics and Public Policy (Austin 2018, 59). Her experience in serving as the Political Director for Senator Kerry also attracted support from local, state, and federal elected officials (Austin 2018).

In Boston, mayoral elections are every four years and city council elections are every two years including the election for four at-large city councilors to represent the entire city and seven additional city councilors to represent districts within the city. For the at-large city council general election, the top four candidates to receive the most votes are elected. Despite a crowded field including eight candidates in the general election and even more in the primary election, Pressley scored 41,879 votes and ranked 4th among eight City Councilor At-Large candidates in the general election to become one of the city's four City Councilors At-Large (Seelye and Herndon 2018). In her first political race, Pressley achieved a historic first by becoming the first woman of color to be elected to the Boston City Council.

As City Councilor At-Large, Pressley swiftly transitioned from campaigning to governing. She established and chaired the City Council's Committee on Healthy Women, Families, and Communities. The committee focused on stabilizing families and communities, preventing violence and trauma, combatting poverty, and addressing issues like teenage pregnancy and health education, as well as abortion rights. Additionally, she pressed the Boston Public Schools to implement a comprehensive curriculum for sex education.

Pressley led with issues she believed mattered to voters and correspondingly increased her likeability among constituents. As a result, she garnered the most votes for re-election in 2011, 2013, and 2015; and the second highest votes in 2017. This feat marked the first time in Boston's history that a person of color and a woman achieved such an outstanding record of support as a member of the Boston City Council (Seelye and Herndon 2018). It was no easy accomplishment especially in her second re-election campaign. In the summer prior to the 2013 primary election, Pressley's mother passed away from leukemia. As her mother became increasingly ill, Pressley became less present in city council meetings and on the campaign trail. But her community of Boston voters showed their support for Pressley at the polls. In the end, she came in first among candidates in more than half of Boston's 22 wards. She garnered 85 percent of the votes by Black/African-Americans in the neighborhoods of Roxbury, Jamaica Plain, and Roslindale, and even came in second among candidates in the mostly white neighborhood of West Roxbury (Austin 2018). See Figure 4.1 for total votes received by Pressley for city council.

Despite Pressley's historic firsts and that of Governor Patrick among others, people of color as well as women remain grossly underrepresented in Massachusetts state and local government. According to a 2019 MassINC study, white residents are overrepresented in the State Legislature by approximately 16 percent, with 31 additional members of color needing to be elected to properly represent Asian,

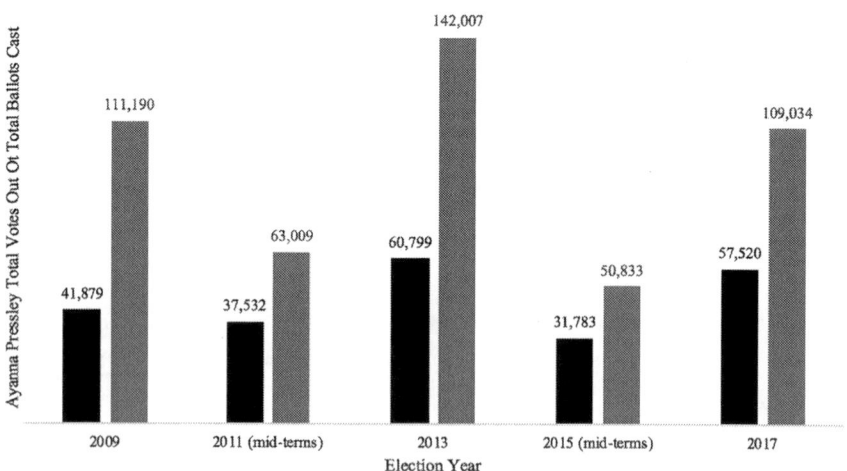

FIGURE 4.1 Ayanna Pressley Total Votes Received Out of Total Ballots Cast Boston City Councilor At-Large (2009–2017)

City of Boston, Elections Department, 2009–2017

African-American, and Latino residents (Levine, Foreman, and Bliss 2019). Similar disparities exist among women in state politics. While 52 percent of adult residents are women, the Massachusetts State Legislature is comprised of less than 29 percent women (Levine, Forman, and Bliss 2019). The Massachusetts State Legislature led a statewide redistricting plan after the 2010 U.S. Census and shifted from eleven to ten congressional seats (Thys 2010). Redistricting resulted in the first majority-minority district in Massachusetts, the 7th Congressional District (Koczela 2018). Formerly considered the Massachusetts 8th Congressional District, this newly created district was comprised of 40.8 percent white residents compared to the 70.7 percent white residents across the state. As such, it left advocates hopeful that it would increase diversity among state elected officials and spark greater influence within neighborhoods of color (Salsberg 2016).

The Massachusetts 7th Congressional District is comprised mostly of Boston along with parts of Cambridge and the town of Milton as well as the cities of Chelsea, Everett, and Somerville and the town of Randolph. Leading up to its first election in 2012, this metropolitan electorate was more diverse and less clearly defined than in the past by people of color—including Black, Latino, and Asian residents—who comprised 56 percent of residents from the cities of Somerville, Chelsea, and Everett, a third of the town of Milton, half of the city of Cambridge, and much of the city of Boston (Miller 2018b). In Boston, alone, 28.9 percent of residents are foreign born with significant representation from China, Dominican Republic, Haiti, Vietnam, El Salvador, Cape Verde among other Latin, Asian, and European countries, and of the foreign-born residents, 46 percent are naturalized citizens (Lima et al. 2018).

Pressley's Opposition: Congressman Michael Capuano

By 2018, the 7th Congressional District (and its former, the 8th Congressional District) had been served by Congressman Michael Capuano for ten consecutive terms. Before serving in Congress for nearly 20 years, Capuano was first an alderman, then mayor for almost 10 years in the city of Somerville—a 4.1 square mile municipality that is a part of the 7th Congressional District and abuts the cities of Boston and Cambridge. Capuano was born to first-generation Irish and Italian immigrants in Somerville in 1952, over two decades before Pressley was born (DeCosta-Klipa 2018). Capuano graduated from Dartmouth College in New Hampshire before returning to Boston to earn his law degree at Boston College Law School (DeCosta-Klipa 2018). He first entered local politics by serving on his hometown's Board of Alderman. Capuano attempted three times to run for mayor of the city of Somerville, finally winning with his third campaign in 1989 (DeCosta-Klipa 2018). As mayor, he continued to pursue higher office. By 1998, Congressman Joe Kennedy II's seat opened, and Capuano entered a crowded race with ten candidates; he successfully won his inaugural congressional race to represent his hometown and surrounding communities in the U.S. House of Representatives (DeCosta-Klipa 2018). As a U.S. Congressman, Capuano was an active member of the Congressional Progressive Caucus (DeCosta-Klipa 2018).

During his 20 years representing the district, Capuano was notably outspoken including his stance against Wall Street during the Great Recession and his votes against the Iraq War and the No Child Left Behind education bill (DeCosta-Klipa 2018). He even sued the administrations of President George W. Bush and President Barack Obama, standing up against the presidents' executive war powers (DeCosta-Klipa 2018). As a bold, progressive leader in Congress, Capuano maintained likeability within the district evidenced by the fact he never faced opposition within the Democratic party in any of his re-elections prior to 2018 (MA Election Statistics 2018). According to non-partisan studies of his voting record, he also remained true to his progressive values with a pattern of voting on the left (Pindell 2018). His 2018 re-election campaign press secretary described Capuano as "an unwavering fighter for progressive values who is taking on Donald Trump at every turn and working hard for the people he represents" (Pindell 2018).

Pressley Versus Capuano

In Massachusetts, opponents from each political party square off in primary elections, then the winning candidate from each party competes against each other in the general election on the first Tuesday in November of election year. For the Massachusetts 7th Congressional District, the only candidates in the race were Capuano and Pressley, both Democrats; therefore, whoever won the primary would be the presumptive winner to represent the district in the U.S. House of Representatives. The head-to-head campaign between Pressley and Capuano spanned roughly eight months, leading up to the primary election on September 4, 2018. With the Massachusetts primary election serving as the standoff between the only two candidates for the 7th Congressional District, all eyes were waiting for the results the evening of the primary election not only locally but nationally, too. Soon after polls closed, it was confirmed that Pressley defeated Capuano by a landslide, beating the long-term incumbent by 17.2 percentage points (MA Election Stats). Pressley successfully earned 58.5 percent of the votes compared to Capuano who only secured 41.3 percent of the 106,556 total ballots cast (MA Election Stats). After her primary win and a general election without opposition, Pressley went on to become the first Black woman from Massachusetts elected to the U.S. Congress and the first person of color to represent the Massachusetts 7th Congressional District. See Table 4.1 for primary results.

How did Pressley's campaign secure her victory? By way of background, there was a political outcry that had swarmed the nation by 2018. It was apparent not only in Boston but districts across the country that there was a lack of Black and women political leaders. Several successful campaigns emerged in 2018—locally,

TABLE 4.1 2018 U.S. House Democratic Primary: Massachusetts 7th Congressional District

City/Town	Pressley	Capuano	All Others	Blanks	Total Votes Cast
Boston	40,615	22,914	127	2,800	66,456
Cambridge	6,029	4,655	7	185	10,876
Chelsea	968	1,139	0	128	2,235
Everett	1,498	2,804	11	471	4,784
Milton	815	606	1	33	1,455
Randolph	1,835	1,889	4	93	3,821
Somerville	8,286	8,423	22	198	16,929
TOTAL	60,046	42,430	172	3,908	106,556

Source: Massachusetts Election Statistics, Secretary of the Commonwealth 2018.

Massachusetts District Attorney Rachel Rollins of Suffolk County, and nationally, Alexandria Ocasio-Cortez, who ran for the U.S. House of Representatives against an incumbent in the New York Democratic primary, and Ilhan Omar, who launched a congressional campaign after the Democratic incumbent representing her district chose not to seek re-election in Minnesota. Additionally, "times up" and "me too" national movements were widespread when a groundswell of women began speaking out and up for themselves after years of harassment and assault in politics as well as media, entertainment, sports, and other industries. By 2018, protests had become commonplace in Boston and across the country, rallying to protect the rights of women, Black lives, immigrants, LGBTQ communities and more. In Massachusetts, known for its liberal politics, City Councilor Pressley and Congressman Capuano were among the most vocal leaders that joined rallies and demonstrations in support of these communities.

In 2018, Pressley felt like it was her turn. The year prior, Pressley visited her father, who retired in North Carolina following a career with the United Negro College Fund years after prison, to share her hopes and vision in pursuing higher office (Levenson and Ebbert 2018). Since her first campaign for city council, there had been several changes in her life. Pressley's mother had passed away in 2013. Pressley married Conan Harris in 2014 and became a stepmother or what she affectionately calls "bonus mom" to his daughter. Pressley first met Harris in her early years as a city councilor when he worked for a violence prevention program. Harris went on to join the city of Boston in the Mayor's Office of Public Safety, and My Brother's Keeper local initiative (Levenson and Ebbert 2018). Pressley was not motivated to run for higher office because of the national political climate, nor the presidential election of Donald Trump; rather, she was motivated to tackle the systemic inequalities and disparities she had long talked about in Boston—well before as she put it "that man occupied the White House!" (Seelye and Herndon 2018).

In January 2018, Pressley announced her campaign to run for the 7th Congressional District against Democrat and 20-year incumbent Congressman Michael Capuano. Within days of her announcement, race and gender became a focal point on the campaign trail. That same month, Capuano and Pressley were interviewed separately by WBoston University Radio, Boston's National Public Radio station. During this radio interview, Capuano admitted that identity can influence a voter's choice though there are many other deciding factors; nevertheless, he quipped: "I cannot be a woman of color" (Miller 2018b). While Capuano stated the obvious, he goes onto acknowledge the implicit, unspoken role race and gender can play in the campaign environment. Capuano expressed that he did not think voters would weigh their decision to vote or not vote for him because he is white and male (Miller 2018b). Still, Pressley was his first opponent in a Democratic primary since becoming a congressman in 1998 and he was quick to point out her race and gender. His remarks could have easily been received negatively and labeled offensive by listeners.

Given the degree of uncertainty associated with this electoral contest, media messaging took on additional importance particularly in terms of content. As in most biracial electoral contests, the media as well as white opponent—that being, in this case: Capuano—could inject race and gender in extraordinary ways. His remarks could be thought of, in a most general sense, as an effort to minimize perceived political risk when considering the demographic makeup of the 7th Congressional district in Massachusetts. In response, Pressley employed group-oriented rhetoric and identity-based appeals. Thus, her multiple group identity became a strategic resource from which she could reap votes.

In a separate interview with the same WBUR reporter, Pressley acknowledged she and Capuano shared progressive values but asserted that she would bring a different lens to the same political issues (Miller 2018b). Though she acknowledged everyone has their own perspective in life, she astutely shared "when you have issues that are being developed through a completely monolithic and homogenized prism, everyone suffers for that" (Miller 2018b). Pressley continued to drive this message home to Massachusetts' only majority-minority congressional district through the control of campaign communications from broad and narrow-cast messages to sociocultural cues as well as language. Both her race (Blackness) and gender (female) became deployable, reputational assets that provided certain tangible and intangible benefits not available to her opponent on account of his whiteness and maleness. Pressley's race and gender went from passive attributes to elevated resources when emphasized on the campaign trail. Pressley could do so based on a set of assumptions regarding political representation used to critique her opponent and assume the upper hand.

Notably, Pressley held her campaign launch in Cambridge, outside of her home turf of Boston, at a restaurant filled with over 300 people in early February (Bay State Banner 2018). As she engaged with supporters, Pressley vowed to work on issues, such as increasing health care costs, the gap of income inequality, access to capital for small businesses, and the lack of affordable housing (Bay State Banner 2018). Despite being in her fifth term as city councilor and one of the most popular of the city councilors in Boston, Pressley still had to formally introduce herself as a congressional candidate to the majority of Boston as well as half of the city of Cambridge, one-third of the town of Milton, and the cities of Somerville, Chelsea, and Everett, and the town of Randolph—all comprising the 7th Congressional District and all-too familiar for Capuano's campaign. Though they shared similar progressive values, Pressley had to distinguish herself from Capuano and tailor her message to appeal to white and minority constituencies alike using a toggling approach. Stressing that voting as a progressive would not lead to progress, Pressley alleged that she could lead in new ways on account of her personal biography and unique angle of vision as a Black woman with a multi-track strategy whereby race and gender could be at once emphasized and de-emphasized by this historic first candidate to mobilize a given constituency (Collet 2008; Catanese 2018).

By the time of her campaign launch event, WBUR released a poll that surveyed likely Democrats and showed Capuano with a 12 percent lead over Pressley districtwide (Bay State Banner 2018). However, this same poll indicated Pressley held an 11 percent lead over Capuano in Boston (Bay State Banner 2018). But, six months into the campaign, Pressley faced the same question repeatedly: what sets Pressley apart from Capuano? Capuano, a 66-year-old white man who had served the district for nearly 20 years, had the advantage of always referring to his congressional voting record, advocacy on progressive policies, and seniority to offer greater influence within the gridlock elected officials often encountered in the U.S. House of Representatives (Levenson 2018). When it came to policies and values, Pressley and Capuano arguably shared too similar of positions to strike a contrast that resonated with voters (Levenson 2018).

Both campaigns could debate the impact of votes versus advocacy, and small differences on positions like abortion and gun control; yet these differences were quite miniscule for the average voter to differentiate between two liberal, progressive candidates. Pressley, for example, explained on the campaign trail that she would advocate even more than Capuano had done to repeal the Hyde Amendment, which bans federal funding of most abortions (Levenson 2018). Capuano, however, quickly defended his record in opposition of this amendment and the longtime effort by Congress in attempt to repeal it, coupled by a supportive statement from a Connecticut congresswoman who underscored Capuano's leadership in protecting and advocating for women's rights (Levenson 2018). Since policy differences would not be the game changer in this campaign, it made it difficult for the average voter to distinguish between the two candidates based on policy preferences alone (Levenson 2018). So much so that on the eve of the September primary, *The New York Times* declared that the primary results will be a testament to political organizing and "whether voters in the racially diverse district prefer a black woman to the white male incumbent" (Herndon 2018).

So how did Pressley transition from lagging in the polls to a landslide victory in the primary election? Pressley worked hard at identifying with voters by emphasizing her personal biography as much as her policy stands to win election. She had the instinctive ability to establish trust across racial and ethnic constituencies by virtue of her experiences with these communities, knowledge of their norms, languages, and cultural practices, including deep connections with key political actors.

Over the course of her eight-month campaign, Pressley positioned herself as change agent often preaching *change can't wait* as her campaign slogan on issues that not only women or people of color could relate to, but issues that impacted approximately 800,000 residents of the district regardless of gender or race. From underscoring this message in speeches to creating trending hashtags, the message of *change can't wait* began to resonate among her supporters on the campaign trail. Her public visibility raised the salience of multiple group identities—age, race, ethnicity, and gender—shared by the demographic majority in Boston. For this district, 20.8 percent were Black or African-American residents and another 20.2 percent were Hispanic or Latino residents (U.S. Census Bureau 2018). Besides this, women were 52 percent of the district's population and a younger cohort between the ages of 20 and 49 (like Pressley) constituted 54 percent of all residents, and another 25 percent of all residents between the ages of 20 and 29 years old, were not of voting age or even born when Capuano first took office (Census Reporter).

Nevertheless, with Capuano's seniority and favorability in Congress, he secured several key endorsements during the campaign including local leaders such as Mayor Marty Walsh of Boston and former Massachusetts Governor Deval Patrick as well as such national congressmen and women of color as U.S. House Representatives John Lewis of Georgia, and Maxine Waters of California plus the Congressional Black Caucus Political Action Committee (Seelye and Herndon 2018; Dezenski 2018). In March, Congressman John Lewis described Capuano as a "champion" and "fierce advocate for those who have often been forgotten or left behind," crediting Capuano for his track record on issues including income inequality, civil rights, gun control, health care, affordable housing, gender pay equity, immigration, or transportation (Miller 2018a).

Even though Pressley did not have the Boston-bred pedigree, she did not let that become a disadvantage when enlisting endorsements. In fact, there had been a yearning for change in the city and the state of Massachusetts. It helped that the state's Attorney General Maura Healey recognized that shift in perspectives. Upon endorsing Pressley, Attorney General Healey described Pressley as someone who "really can speak to people and speak to issues that are real to people" (Catanese 2018). While many elected officials in the Massachusetts congressional delegation remained neutral during the race, like Senator Elizabeth Warren, Pressley did earn the endorsement from her city council peers including councilors Annissa Essaibi George, Michelle Wu, and Kim Janey along with a contingent of state and local legislators in the Greater Boston region (DeCosta-Klipa 2018). Pressley also received endorsements on the national level from Indivisible, an anti-Trump grassroots organization, and the National Women's Political Caucus (DeCosta-Klipa 2018). *The Boston Globe* and *The Boston Herald* typically share editorial board endorsements approximately a week prior to an election, and just before the primary, both outlets endorsed Pressley (DeCosta-Klipa 2018). In its editorial, *The Boston Globe* touted Pressley's "creative approach to reducing inequality is the mindset the district needs" as well as her ability to be "an advocate in touch with the everyday experiences of the district's residents, including the most vulnerable" (Boston Globe Editorial Board 2018).

Roughly one month prior to the September primary election, Capuano maintained a 13-point lead based on a poll conducted by WBUR of 403 likely voters in the district over three days in late July (Seelye and Herndon 2018). Pollsters suggested Pressley could take the lead if she secured an increase in voter turnout among non-white as well as young voters (Thys 2018). Why was this important? This WBUR poll reported that while most likely voters did not think gender would impact vote choice, most registered voters believed race was a major or at least minor consideration that may influence vote choice (Thys 2018). While the 7th Congressional District is comprised of mostly non-white residents, this majority were not registered voters or among those who habitually turnout. And so, the same WBUR poll that reported Capuano's lead also showed Pressley with a 23-point lead against Capuano among African-American registered voters (Thys 2018). These poll results were significant—for example, when reviewing voter turnout in 2014—the immediate past mid-term election cycle—65 percent of votes were cast by white voters despite white residents only accounting for 42 percent of the population (Koczela 2018). This known disparity between the demographic makeup of residents who were registered voters or voting eligible and those registered who cast votes afforded Pressley an opportunity. She would engage previously inactive voters or residents who had not yet registered but who were eligible to vote in the primary election. And so, Pressley ceased upon this opportunity as a veteran campaigner. She capitalized on her past experiences, connecting with voters as both a candidate for city council and campaign volunteer working on U.S. Senator John Kerry's re-election bid.

Building off her successful "100 Club" campaign strategy as a candidate for city council, she tapped other respected leaders to attract new voters, mobilize existing voters, and get out the vote across the district. By April, the campaign had activated more than 300 volunteers throughout the district (Daniel 2018). Among campaign volunteers included City Council President Damali Vidot of Chelsea, who also endorsed Pressley and hit the trail with over 40 volunteers on the campaign's first "Day of Action" in the early spring (Daniel 2018). She opined that "leadership like Ayanna's is what our country is missing at this critical moment in history" and called for "representatives that will lead with us, for us, and alongside us to help build the communities we deserve" (Daniel 2018). In addition to coalition building municipality by municipality within the district, Pressley also organized support among ethnic groups in the community. Recognizing the significant Haitian community in Boston, Pressley tapped Marie St. Fleur, a former Massachusetts State Representative and Haitian from the Boston neighborhood of Dorchester, to rally support among the Boston area Haitian community (Catanese 2018), a task St. Fleur had also done during Senator Kerry's campaign (Austin 2018, 40). Given St. Fleur's credibility with Haitians, there was an ease in putting out a call to action within this group. During a weekend campaign stop, Pressley joined St. Fleur for a community event in which St. Fleur said: "When you leave here today, I ask for you to take [Pressley's] energy" (Catanese 2018). Events like this one and others energized demographic groups, neighborhoods, and communities that had been traditionally or previously overlooked by candidates running for office.

To garner more votes and increase political engagement, Pressley relied heavily on social media platforms to reach a new generation of supporters and make the campaign more accessible (Scott 2018). While Capuano had the incumbent advantage, Pressley took the position that "a young and majority-minority district needed a fresh voice in Washington" (Scott 2018). Her own personal life story afforded her credibility with a demographic she aimed to represent and, at the same time, shored up her commitment to fight for the underdog, as she declared "I fundamentally believe that the people closest to the pain should be closest to the power" (Scott 2018). A strategy that had proven effective in her past campaigns, Pressley's social media posts often cited the hashtag #ChangeCantWait as her growing followers engaged in conversation and expressed support by reciting the theme of her campaign repeatedly (Martinez 2018).

Both the courtship, and active use, of both free and paid ethnic media was a vitally important campaign resource. It tied those who otherwise may have remained out of reach due to language barriers to the campaign with minimal risk of alienating out-group (read: white) voters—for example, 37 percent of Boston residents speak a second language other than English at home. She introduced herself to these prospective voters by expanding her campaign communications to include Spanish, Haitian, Chinese, and African-American media outlets. The campaign ran media advertisements in Spanish on Telemundo and Univision that featured local Latino community members who voiced their support (Martinez 2018). Such a campaign communications strategy was clever, with Spanish being the most common language other than English spoken by Boston residents (Lima et al. 2018). Josiane Martinez, architect of the campaign's multilingual communications strategy, credits examples like this in drawing "tens of thousands of new voters" to the primary election (Martinez 2018).

A Breakdown of Results

The Massachusetts 7th Congressional District experienced a significant increase in voter turnout during the 2018 primary election. This election attracted more voters compared to the immediate past mid-term election. When Capuano ran unopposed in 2014 only 61,725 votes were counted compared to 106,556 ballots cast in 2018 (MA Election Statistics 2018). Consistent with national trends, the district experienced a major spike in turnout among Black voters, representing 23 percent of district turnout compared to only 4 percent of turnout in all other Massachusetts primaries, which also have significantly less Black residents and voters (Duggan 2019). Still, white voters constituted most voters in this diverse congressional district—specifically, 55 percent of first-time voters and 63 percent of habitual voters in the district were white in this election (Duggan 2019). While 50 percent of voters were first-time voters in the 7th Congressional District primary election, 24 percent of voters had not voted previously in any of the past five presidential primaries (Duggan 2019). According to analysis provided by WBUR, the 24 percent of first-time voters included 55 percent women and 66 percent between the ages of 18 to 44 years. Of the 66 percent between 18 and 44 years old, 34 percent were between the ages of 18 to 29 years old. Of this younger cohort, 20 percent were women, representing the most significant population among these new voters.

Conclusion

Ayanna Pressley has been making history ever since her first city council race in 2009. Pressley's win in 2018 broke yet another glass ceiling as she became the first Black woman from Massachusetts elected to the U.S. Congress, and the first woman and person of color to represent 7th Congressional District. Pressley's win symbolizes another step forward for women and people of color in Massachusetts. Historic first candidates like Pressley lay the groundwork for rising political elites (Simien 2015). While the way in which Pressley's public visibility raised the salience of group identities—age, race, ethnicity, and gender—is significant and meaningful, it is equally important to recognize that historic first candidates like herself want members of their home district to recognize them as one of them based on policy interests, not simply their physical characteristics.

Recalling the WBUR interview at the start of the campaign when Capuano said he could never be a Black woman, Pressley made it clear to potential voters sitting in pews at the Old South Meeting House in Boston,

> I am Black, and I am a woman. And I embrace both of those facts. But to suggest that the only difference is my race, and my gender is wrong and

toxic. And the voters of the 7th Congressional District aren't buying it. The issues I have worked on my entire life transcend my identity.

Dezenski and Griffiths 2018

In another interview during the campaign, Pressley shared:

I've never asked anyone to vote for me because I'm black and a woman. I'm asking people to consider me because I'm pledging to be a vote, a voice, and a partner. I'm asking people to vote for me because I'm an activist leader and a problem solver.

Though Pressley did not base her campaign solely on identity politics, it was a visible contrast between her and her opponent, allowing residents especially women, young adults, and Black residents to see someone for the first time "stand for" them on the campaign trail. Pressley reminded voters that "change can't wait" and this slogan should not be overlooked or forgotten.

As the chant "change can't wait" roared through the crowd the night of the general election on November 6, 2018, Pressley stood with poise and ease at the podium. In her acceptance speech, Pressley reflected on the evening—a historic victory not only for herself but women candidates across Massachusetts and the country. As she addressed what she described as her "broad and diverse coalition of voters, disrupters, believers, resisters, persisters, activists, and agitators" she emphatically stated she knew "for a fact none of us ran to make history. We ran to make change." That said, Pressley joins women of color elected to public office in 2018 who promised to uphold an agenda to fight for social, economic, and political justice (Perry 2019). The landmark victory for Congresswoman Pressley demonstrates that historic first candidates can achieve representation under conditions that may otherwise discourage their candidacy (read: incumbency advantage). Fortunately for Pressley, descriptive and symbolic representation mattered as much as substantive representation for constituents of the 7th Congressional District of Massachusetts.

Although it has sparked much debate, intersectionality research has, to its credit, brought to the fore intersectional actors and generated a deeper appreciation for historic first candidates like Pressley and how their identities inform campaigns. The role that race, and gender play in mobilizing such diverse electorates are understudied facets of American elections (as are historic first candidacies). A more comprehensive study of American political behavior would include support for historic firsts. The utility of such an approach cannot be overstated, given that it affords those who study campaigns and elections a remarkable opportunity to expand the theoretical capacity of intersectionality research by studying the role of identities (plural) in determining political behaviors, and electoral outcomes as shown here.

Note

1 This 2015 data comes from the Boston Planning and Development Agency.

References

Austin, Sharon D. Wright. 2018. *The Caribbeanization of Black Politics: Race, Group Consciousness, and Political Participation in America.* Albany, NY: State University of New York Press.

Bay State Banner 2018. "Pressley Launches Bid for Congressional Seat." *Bay State Banner*, February 21, 2018. www.baystatebanner.com/2018/02/21/pressley-launches-bid-for-congressional-seat/

BPDA. 2017. "Neighborhood Profiles." Boston Planning and Development Agency, August. www.bostonplans.org/getattachment/7987d9b4-193b-4749-8594-e41f1ae27719

BPS Communications Office. 2019. "Boston Public Schools at a Glance." www. bostonpublicschools.org

Catanese, David. "Ayanna Pressley's Fierce Urgency of Now." *U.S News & World Report*, August 10, 2018. www.usnews.com/news/the-report/articles/2018-08-10/ayanna-pressleys- fierce-urgency-of-now

City of Boston, Elections Department, Archived Election Results: www.boston.gov/ departments/elections/state-and-city-election-results.

Collet, Christian. 2008. "Minority Candidates, Alternative Media, and Multiethnic America: Deracialization or Toggling?" *Perspectives on Politics* 6(4): 707–728.

Daniel, Seth. 2018. "Council President Endorses Pressley, Capuano Touts Fundraising." *Chelsea Record*, April 6, 2018. http://chelsearecord.com/2018/04/06/council-president-endorses-pressleycapuano-touts-fundraising/

DeCosta-Klipa, Nik. 2018. "Everything you need to know about Ayanna Pressley." Boston.com. August 31, 2018. www.boston.com/news/politics/2018/08/31/ayanna-pressley-massachusetts-primary

Dezenski, Lauren, and Brett D. Griffiths. 2018. "Pressley's Counterpoint- UMass Boston Shakeup." *Politico*, May 22, 2018.

Duggan, Maeve. 2019. "24 Percent Of 7th District Primary Voters Had Not Voted in Previous 5 Primaries." WBUR, January 4. www.wbur.org/news/2019/01/04/ayanna-pressley-first-time-voter-file-analysis

Dezenski, Laura. 2018. "CBC Endorses Capuano in Massachusetts Democratic Primary." *Politico*, May 18, 2018. www.politico.com/story/2018/05/18/michael-capuano-endorsed-cbc-597659

Dovi, Suzanne. 2002. "Preferable Descriptive Representatives: Will Just Any Woman, Black, or Latino Do?" *American Political Science Review* 96 (December): 745–54.

Herndon, Astead W. 2018. "Mike Capuano Is in the Political Fight of His Life." *The NewYorkTimes*, September 3, 2018. www.nytimes.com/2018/09/03/us/politics/capuano-massachusetts-primary.html

Irons, Meghan E., Shelley Murphy, and Jenna Russell. 2014. "History rolled in on a yellow school bus." *The Boston Globe*, September 6, 2014. www.bostonglobe.com/metro/2014/09/06/boston-busing-crisis-years-later/DS35nsuqp0yh8f1q9aRQUL/story.html

Koczela, Steve. 2018. "Though the 7th District Is Minority-Majority, Most of Its Voters Are White." WBUR, February 9. www.wbur.org/news/2018/02/09/capuano-pressley-demographics&xid=17259,15700022,15700186,15700191,15700248,15700253

Levenson, Michael. 2018. "Michael Capuano and Ayanna Pressley: What's the difference?" *The Boston Globe*, July 22, 2018. www.bostonglobe.com/metro/2018/07/22/capuano-pressley-grapple-with-same-question-what-makes-you-different/64Uffu4cVVpWZVMYwH4jwL/story.html

Levenson, Michael, and Stephanie Ebbert. 2018. "The life and rise of Ayanna Pressley." *The Boston Globe*, September 8, 2018. www.bostonglobe.com/metro/2018/09/08/the-life-and-rise-ayanna-pressley/pqdppGFPoZPSEwo3Ko23BJ/story.html?event=event12

Levine, Peter, Benjamin Foreman, and Laura Bliss. 2019. "MassForward: Advancing Democratic Innovation and Electoral Reform in Massachusetts." MassINC, November. www.tbf.org/-/media/tbf/reports-and-covers/2019/massforward-report-20191113.pdf?la=en

Lima, Alvaro, et al. 2018. "Boston by the Numbers 2018." Boston Planning and Development Agency. September. www.bostonplans.org/getattachment/3e8bfacf-27c1-4b55-adee-29c5d79f4a38

Martinez, Josiane. 2018. "How Ayanna Pressley Won." WBUR Cognoscenti, Sept 7, 2018.

Massachusetts Election Statistics, Secretary of the Commonwealth of Massachusetts (2018). https://electionstats.state.ma.us/elections/search/year_from:2018/year_to:2018/office_id:5/district_id:58690

Muñoz, Ana Patricia, Marlene Kim, Mariko Chang, Regine O. Jackson, Darrick Hamilton, and William A. Darity Jr. et al. 2015. "The Color of Wealth in Boston: A Joint Publication with Duke University and The New School." Boston, MA: Federal Reserve Bank of Boston.

Miller, Joshua. 2018a. "Civil rights hero John Lewis endorses Mike Capuano." *The Boston Globe,* March 6, 2018. www.bostonglobe.com/metro/2018/03/06/civil-rights-hero-john-lewis-endorses-mike-capuano/ksHpI49c8O5IR7FvY02PyL/story.html

Miller, Joshua. 2018b. "Race, Gender Put Forward As Key Issues In Boston Congressional Race." *The Boston Globe*, February 1, 2018. www.bostonglobe.com/metro/2018/02/01/race-gender-put-forward-key-issues-boston-congressional-race/v6hbmp1cWXFJkgXu3nnj0J/story.html

Perry, Andre M. 2019. "Black Women Are Looking Forward to the 2020 Elections." Brookings Institute, January 10. www.brookings.edu/research/black-women-are-looking-forward-to-the-2020-elections/

Pindell, James. 2018. "Should Ocasio-Cortez's Upset Have Michael Capuano Worried?" *The Boston Globe*, June 27, 2018. www.bostonglobe.com/metro/2018/06/27/after-alexandria-ocasio-cortez-victory-should-mike-capuano

Resilient Cities, July 13. www.adaptationclearinghouse.org/resources/resilient-boston-an-equitable-and-connected-city.html

Ruiz-Grossman, Sarah. 2018. "Ayanna Pressley Will Get the Old Office of Shirley Chisholm, First Black Congresswoman." *Huffington Post,* December 24, 2018. www.huffpost.com/entry/ayanna-pressley-same-office-shirley-chisholm_n_5c1a94a4e4b0ce5184b9c243?guccounter=1

Salsberg, Bob. 2016. "Gains in diversity slow in Massachusetts politics." *Metrowest Daily News*, June 19, 2016. www.metrowestdailynews.com/news/20160619/gains-in-diversity-slow-in-massachusetts-politics.

Schuster, Luc, and Peter Ciurczak. 2018. "Boston's More Diverse Than You May Realize." *Boston Indicators*, September 28. www.bostonindicators.org/article-pages/2018/september/boston-diversity

Scott, Eugene. 2018. "Ayanna Pressley's victory proves it matters to Democratic primary voters 'who those Democrats are." *The Washington Post*, September 5, 2018.

www.washingtonpost.com/politics/2018/09/05/ayanna-pressleys-victory-proves-it-matters-democratic-primary-voters-who-those-democrats-are/

Seelye, Katharine Q., and Astead W. Herndon. 2018. "Ayanna Pressley Seeks Her Political Moment in a Changing Boston." *The New York Times*, September 1, 2018. www.nytimes. com/2018/09/01/us/politics/ayanna-pressley-massachusetts.html

Simien, Evelyn M. 2015. *Historic Firsts: How Symbolic Empowerment Changes U.S. Politics.* New York: Oxford University Press.

Tate, Katherine. 2001. "The Political Representation of Black in Congress: Does Race Matter?" *Legislative Studies Quarterly* 26(4): 623–638.

The Boston Globe Editorial Board, 2018. "Endorsement: Democrats Should Choose Ayanna Pressley for the Seventh District." *The Boston Globe*, August 26, 2018. www. bostonglobe.com/opinion/editorials/2018/08/25/endorsement-democrats-should-choose-ayanna-pressley-for-seventh

Thys, Fred. 2010. "After Losing a House Seat, Someone Must Go." WBUR, December 22. www.wbur.org/news/2010/12/22/ma-loses-a-seat

Thys, Fred. 2018. "WBUR Poll: Capuano Maintains 13-Point Lead Over Pressley." WBUR, August 2. www.wbur.org/news/2018/08/02/wbur-poll-capuano-pressley-7th-district

U.S. Census Bureau. 2018. "Hispanic or Latino Origin by Race American Community Survey 1-year estimates. https://censusreporter.org

5

RASHIDA TLAIB

A Symbol and Champion for Detroit

Michael Minta

In 2018, Rashida Tlaib made history by becoming the first Palestinian American woman elected to the U.S. Congress. She joined Ilhan Omar of Minnesota as the first Muslim woman elected to serve in the highest lawmaking body in the country. Her election was a triumph for Arab Americans, Muslim women, and progressive Democrats who wanted to shake up the Democratic establishment. Tlaib and many other progressives believed that congressional Democrats were not doing enough to impeach and remove President Donald Trump from office. On election night she told a crowd of passionate supporters at a Moveon.org event that she was going to Washington to "impeach the motherfucker," referring to President Donald Trump (Rupar 2019). When rebuked by Republicans and members of her own party, she did not back down. Instead Tlaib tweeted, "she will always speak truth to power" (Rupar 2019). This was not the first time Tlaib confronted Trump—in 2016 she and a group of women were escorted out of the Detroit Economic Club for protesting the president's speech (Hagen 2018). Tlaib, a previously unknown state legislator from Detroit, was now dominating news coverage. Her election provided symbolic empowerment for Arab Americans, Muslims, and women who wanted someone to stand up to President Trump. Historic firsts like Tlaib can heighten the value of participating in electoral politics such as voting, attending campaign rallies, and donating money to campaigns (Simien 2015). Although it is likely that Arab Americans would have voted for a Democrat to stand up to Trump, it was significant that a Palestinian American candidate who shared their ethnic and religious background was on the ballot.

Although much is made about Tlaib being the first Palestinian American woman elected to Congress, what is often understated in these accounts is she campaigned and won in a majority Black district against formidable Black candidates that included Detroit City Council member Brenda Jones and relatives

DOI: 10.4324/9781003213925-5

of her predecessor Rep. John Conyers, Jr., and former Detroit Mayor Coleman Young. Arab Americans and Muslims comprised a small minority of the district population. In 2019, she was one of two non-Blacks to represent such a district, with Rep. Steve Cohen (D-TN) being the other. Tlaib would have to prove her authenticity and commitment, as did Conyers to Blacks, as well as show her commitment to representing progressives, Arab Americans, Muslims, and women. This chapter will examine her rise to power. How did she win in a majority Black district? To what extent were Arab Americans, Muslims, and women symbolically empowered by her 2018 campaign for Congress? This chapter also goes beyond symbolic empowerment and explores how she represents her diverse constituent interests in Congress. I use newspaper accounts, bill sponsorships, and participation in committee oversight hearings to answer these questions. Specifically, the chapter builds upon prior chapters in this volume by providing a complementary perspective on how legislators' descriptive characteristics such as their race, ethnicity, or gender can lead to substantive representation of their constituents.

The Historic Campaign to Replace a Civil Rights Icon

Tlaib's quest to be the first Palestinian and Muslim woman elected to Congress was not an easy feat. In 2018, an opportunity to run for Congress became available when civil rights icon and long-term Congressman John Conyers (D-MI) received immense pressure from party leadership to resign after several former women employees alleged that he engaged in sexual misconduct. Conyers would deny these allegations, but eventually bowed to party pressure and a request by House Speaker Nancy Pelosi to resign from office. Conyers represented the district for over 50 years. The House seat remained vacant for one year after his resignation. Michigan Governor Rick Snyder scheduled a special election for voters to elect a candidate to complete the remaining two months left on Conyers' term to coincide with the regular primary election for the full two-year term. Tlaib, along with a formidable field of challengers, decided to enter both races to compete for the Democratic Party nomination. Of the many people running, three were related to famous Detroit politicians, Coleman Young II—son of Detroit's first Black mayor Coleman Young, Ian Conyers—nephew of John Conyers, and John Conyers III—son of John Conyers. Rep. Conyers would endorse his son as his successor. Despite the name recognition of these candidates, they garnered little support from the Democratic establishment. Even though Conyers III, received his father's endorsement, he was only 27 years of old and had never held elected office. Additionally, in May 2018, the Wayne County clerk disqualified Conyers III from the primary because many of the signatures on the petition that he needed to get on the ballot were not valid signatures. Ironically, the challenge to Conyers III's petition came from his cousin, Ian Conyers (Burke 2018). With one Conyers removed from the ballot, Detroit City Council President Brenda Jones, Bill Wild, mayor of Westfield, and former state House representative Shanelle Jackson were the remaining challengers. Jones was the choice of establishment Democrats with more than 14 years of experience on the city council. She received endorsements from labor unions, clergy, Mayor Mike Duggan, and U.S. Rep. Brenda Lawrence (D-MI). Wild was the only white candidate to challenge for the seat.

Although Tlaib was vying to be the first Palestinian American woman and Muslim woman elected to Congress, she understood the symbolic importance of her candidacy, but did not make it the centerpiece of her campaign. In a 2019 address to a law student association, she acknowledged that most constituents were not aware of the historic nature of her campaign. According to Tlaib,

> They are not caring that I am Muslim, or Palestinian, or a woman. People don't care as much about that as much as national media and people that want to focus on that. You know what they care about? That I share their issues.
>
> *Suchyta 2019*

This is a sound strategy considering that the district, which includes parts of the city of Detroit and the surrounding suburbs, is majority Black and the third poorest in the nation. Table 5.1 shows that the district is 53.6 percent Black, 39.2 percent white, 7.9 percent Latino, and 1.4 percent Asian American. Arab Americans comprise only 5.1 percent of the district, but their percentage is higher than the national average of 0.44 percent. Thus, there was not a need to over-emphasize

TABLE 5.1 Demographics of Michigan U.S. House District 13, State of Michigan, and the United States, 2018

	Michigan's 13th District	*Michigan*	*United States*
Median Age	36.7	39.8	38.2
Percent Bachelor's Degree or Higher	16.5%	29.6%	32.6%
Median Household Income	$34,971	$56,697	$61,937
Percent in Poverty	29.5%	14.1%	13.1%
White	39.2%	80.9%	60.2%
Black	53.6%	15.2%	12.3%
Latino	7.9%	5.1%	18.2%
Asian	1.4%	3.9%	5.5%
Arab American	5.1%	--	0.44%
Foreign Born	7.8%	6.9%	13.6%
Total Population	663,867	9,995,915	327,167,439

Source: U.S. Census, My Congressional District, 116th Congress, www.census.gov/mycd/?st=26&cd=13

ACS Demographic and Housing Estimates, Survey/Program: American Community Survey, 2018: ACS 1-Year Estimates Data Profiles

TableID: DP05 https://data.census.gov/cedsci/table?q=michigan%20race&g=040000US26&tid=ACSDP1Y2018.DP05.

these identities because they might negatively impact her electoral chances, where she might be perceived as being an outsider and not looking after the interests of her majority Black constituency. However, to not acknowledge the importance of her ethnic and religious background could possibly demobilize the excitement of Arab Americans and Muslims about her candidacy. Fortunately for Tlaib, Brenda Jones and none of the other Black opponents made it a campaign explicitly about race or ethnic background. Instead, the Black candidates simply stated they believed they were best suited to continue Conyers' legacy. Perhaps, this was an implicit message to Black constituents meaning that a Black candidate should replace Conyers, but there is not much evidence to suggest a racialized or ethnic campaign. This is in sharp contrast to Rep. Steve Cohen (D-TN), the only other non–Black representing a majority Black district. When Cohen ran to replace the departing Rep. Harold Ford, Jr. (D-TN), he received opposition from the Black clergy and other activists that believed that Blacks should represent the majority Black district that contains the city of Memphis. Tlaib did not experience this open resistance.

Even though Arab Americans are considered white, she identifies as and is visibly a person of color. Also, she is not an outsider. She is the daughter of Palestinian immigrants, but she was born and raised in Detroit. She attended city schools in southwest Detroit. Instead of going away to college, she stayed in Detroit and attended Wayne State University where she earned a bachelors' degree. She would later earn her law degree from Western Michigan University. She is the eldest of 14 children and was the first in her family to attend college. Thus, she understands many of the challenges that affect citizens in her district.

Given the makeup of her district, personal background, extensive history as a community organizer in the area, and her years of service in the state legislature, her campaign focused on economic justice rather traditional civil rights issues. Her outreach in the community and representing them at the state level helped and possibly shielded her from such racial or outsider attacks. She had a strong record on civil rights and fought for marginalized groups. Tlaib won the endorsement of the local major newspaper, the *Detroit Free Press*.

She campaigned on social and economic justice issues. Because she is a Democratic Socialist, her platform includes Medicare for All, a Green New Deal, and climate change. The campaign closely mirrors many issues that she championed when she was in the Michigan state legislature and as a community activist.

Tlaib ran a campaign that was to the left of her main challenger, Brenda Jones. Jones was clearly an establishment candidate who focused on jobs and business development. Jones stated that her campaign platform was like the one she ran on as a Detroit city council member. According to Jones:

My campaign platform is the same urban agenda I have always championed, JONES—Jobs, Opportunities, Neighborhoods, Education and Safety. Now, I will be able to address this platform from a federal perspective. I look forward to ensuring the people of the 13th District are getting their fair share of federal assistance, access to programming and the funding they are entitled to.

Editor 2018

Jones did not make her campaign about going to Washington to serve as a check on Trump. She counted on her name recognition for public service on Detroit's city council.

Although she did not emphasize her heritage in the campaign, Tlaib recognized the importance of her run to the Muslim community: "I didn't run because my election would be historic. I ran because of injustices and because of my boys, who are questioning their [Muslim] identity and whether they belong. I've never been one to stand on the sidelines" (Venkataramanan 2018). Tlaib most likely recognized that in a very closely contested election that turnout by a mobilized Arab American and Muslim community could make a difference between winning and losing. The next section will explore the results of special and regular primary election and the factors that led to her historic win.

Winning and Losing in Michigan House Race of 2018

On August 7, 2018, Rashida Tlaib would win and lose a primary election. She narrowly won the primary election to serve the full two-year term. Of the 89,321 votes received Tlaib garnered 31.17 percent; Jones, 30.16 percent; Wild, 14.1 percent; Young, 12.51 percent; Conyers, 6.57 percent; and Shanelle Jackson, 5.43 percent (see Table 5.2) for results. Tlaib received only 900 votes more than her closest competitor Brenda Jones. In the contest to fill the unexpired term, Tlaib lost to

TABLE 5.2 2018 Michigan Election Results, U.S. House, 13th District

Candidates and Party Affiliation (excluding write-ins)	Primary Election— Full term	Special Election— Unexpired Term	General Election— Full Term
Rashida Tlaib-Democrat	31.17%	35.85%	84.24%
*Brenda Jones-Democrat	30.16%	37.75%	0.32%
Bill Wild-Democrat	14.12%	15.17%	---
Coleman A. Young II-Democrat	12.51%	------	---
Ian Conyers-Democrat	6.57%	11.23%	---
Shanelle Jackson-Democrat	5.43%	------	----
Sam Johnson-Working Class			11.30%
Etta Wilcox-Green			4.07%
Total Votes	89,321	86,815	196,299

Source: State of Michigan, Department of State, 2018 Michigan Election Results, Primary, August 8, 2018.

* Brenda Jones ran as a Write-in candidate in the general election.

Brenda Jones by 1648 votes. Of the 86,815 votes cast, Jones received 37.75 percent and Tlaib received 35.85 percent. What factors explain these unusual results? Why did Tlaib win the Democratic primary for the full two-year term election but lost the chance to finish the remaining two months of the unexpired term? First, the election deciding the full term had more candidates than the election dealing with the unexpired term. The full-term election had six candidates and two write-ins compared to four candidates and two write-ins, with Coleman Young II only competing in the contest to serve the full term. Thus, Young's decision not run for the unexpired term allowed Jones to consolidate the Black vote and win the contest. When Young stayed in the contest, Blacks split the vote and allowed Tlaib to win the contest for the full term. Since the district was overwhelmingly Democratic, the winner of the primary was favored to win the seat. Republicans did not even run a candidate in the general election. Tlaib easily won the general election with 84.24 percent of the 196,299 ballots cast with Sam Johnson of the Working-Class Party coming in second with 11.3 percent. Brenda Jones and John Conyers, III, would run in the general election as write-in candidates but combined received less 0.5 percent of the vote.

Tlaib benefitted from the crowded field of African-American candidates splitting the Black vote, but there are many other factors that contributed to her historic victory. First, she is no stranger to running and winning in tough electoral competitions. In 2008, she ran for a seat in the Michigan state House in a crowded field of Black and Latino candidates in a majority Latino and Black district. She won the primary and general election, becoming the first Muslim woman to serve in the Michigan state legislature. In 2011, she faced another tough electoral competition when her district was redrawn after a redistricting cycle and combined with another formidable African-American incumbent, Maureen Stapleton of Detroit. Stapleton was a long-time state House representative with strong support in the Black community. Tlaib won that race also, but she could not run for a fourth term due to term limits. Instead Tlaib ran for the state senate but lost in the Democratic primary to the African-American incumbent, Virgil Smith. Aside from the loss to Smith, Tlaib has a record of success in running and competing against Black candidates in majority Black and Latino districts.

Second, even though the election was local, Tlaib was part of several national forces that helped push her victory. The Trump administration's fight against immigrants and travel bans on Muslim countries sparked a massive resistance. As Trump denounced Muslims, a record number of Muslim candidates ran for political office, including Ilhan Omar of Minnesota. These candidates were supported by groups such as the Council on American-Islamic Relations (CAIR) and Empowering Engaged Muslims, which are the two major groups in the United States responsible for recruiting and funding Muslim candidates. Another Muslim candidate in Michigan, Fayrouz Saad, ran for a U.S. House seat in the Detroit area, but lost in the primary. The big difference in electoral prospects between the two candidates was that Tlaib ran in a district that Hillary Clinton won by

32 percentage points in the 2016 presidential election and Saad ran in a district where Trump won by four percentage points. Tlaib's chances to win would be determined primarily in the Democratic primary. Additionally, Donald Trump's mistreatment of women led to protests by women against him. Tlaib led a protest at one of Trump's events and was forcibly removed by his security. The action garnered national support and recognition for Tlaib, even earning her financial support from Emily's List. Tlaib's ability to link her election to a national struggle explains her massive fundraising advantage over her opponents. Table 5.3 shows that Tlaib raised the most money of all the candidates. Tlaib raised $1.6 million followed by Bill Wild at $637,256 and Brenda Jones at $269,838. Candidates that raise the most money usually win in congressional elections. Tlaib needed the money because she was running in a majority Black district against a mostly Black candidate field. Again, a field populated by Brenda Jones, Ian Conyers, and Coleman Young II. Tlaib received individual campaign contributions from groups such as Moveon.org with $11,793, Eagle Canyon Capital, $15,000, United Food and Commercial Works Union, $12,500, Emily's List, $8,735, and Justice Democrats, $6,997. Brenda Jones received most of her campaign contributions from unions, $10,000 each from the United Auto Workers and Carpenters and Joiners Union. She also received $10,000 from TCF Financial.

Tlaib's financial advantage was even greater when factoring in money spent by outside interest groups on the campaign. Table 5.4 shows that independent groups spent almost $30,000 supporting her campaign while Jones and Ian Conyers combined received less than $1700 in support of their campaigns. These

TABLE 5.3 Money Raised in Michigan District 13, Special Election 2018

Candidate	Money Raised
Rashida Tlaib	$1,625,783
Bill Wild	$637,256
Brenda Jones	$269,838
Ian Conyers	$212,375

Source: Center for Responsive Politics, Politicians & Elections, Congressional Races, Michigan.

TABLE 5.4 Outside Spending by Independent Groups in Michigan District 13 Special Election, 2018

Candidate	Supported	Opposed
Rashida Tlaib	$29,377	$8,225
Brenda Jones	$146	$0
Ian Conyers	$1,470	$0

Source: Center for Responsive Politics, www.opensecrets.org/races/outside-spending?cycle= 2018&id=MI13&spec=Y.

independent groups were not affiliated with Tlaib's campaign, but they can spend money to buy ads supporting or opposing candidates. Moveon.org spent $18,830 in buying ads to support her. The independent expenditures against Tlaib came in the general election when the American Principles Super Pac spent $8225 opposing her candidacy.

Much of Tlaib's campaign donations came from outside of Michigan demonstrating the national appeal and significance of her campaign. More than 73 percent, or $896,556, of Tlaib's campaign funds came from outside of the state while only 26.8 percent, or $328,511, came from in-state. Most candidates for the House of Representatives receive most of their money from in-state contributors. Her challengers received most of their funding from in-state sources—93.4 percent for Wild and 78.8 percent for Jones (Center for Responsive Politics, Politicians and Election 2018). The large influx of out-of-state funds may be due in part to Tlaib's campaign focus to impeach President Donald Trump. In an interview with *The Hill*, Tlaib said "I keep telling people this is about electing a jury that will impeach him, and I make a heck of a juror" (Hagen 2018). Despite outraising all candidates, she only won by 900 votes and lost the election to fill the remainder of Conyers' term.

Finally, Tlaib credits her grassroots campaign for making the difference in her electoral victory. The campaign goal was to knock on at least 50,000 doors. According to her campaign manager, Andy Goddeeris, Tlaib personally knocked on more than 5000 doors, assisted by a diverse team of ten young people, asking constituents for their support (Burke, Ferretti, and Noble 2018). From the existing review of newspapers accounts, it does not appear that other candidates mounted a similar campaign. According to Godderris, the campaign goal was to get Arab Americans to the polls, many who were interested in getting involved since Trump's victory in 2016. Considering that Tlaib won by less than 900 votes, efforts to mobilize Arab American voters most likely played an important role in her victory. Places in the district with high concentrations of Arab Americans like Dearborn and Dearborn Heights were predicted to have higher than normal voter turnout. Thus, having an Arab American on the ticket combined with her promise to impeach Trump were significant in helping her win the two-year term.

Victory and Symbolic Empowerment

Rashida Tlaib's historic victory inspired Arab Americans, Muslims, and Muslim women. In 2019, when she was sworn into Congress, instead of taking the oath of office on the Bible like the overwhelming number of members, she took it on the Qur'an wearing a traditional Palestinian thobe. Many Muslim women posted pictures of themselves wearing a thobe on social media (Brennan 2019). This demonstrates the symbolic empowerment of historic firsts (Simien 2015). A newspaper publisher for the Dearborn-based *The Arab American News*, Oussama Siblani said that Tlaib's victory was significant for the Arab American community.

Additionally, her victory along with Ilhan Omar's victory marked a turning point for a country in its recognition of its Muslim citizens. To Tlaib and other progressives, their swearing-in indicated the nation's rejection of Trump's Muslim ban—a ban that was based on negative stereotypes of Muslims being terrorists. According to Siblani,

> Muslim Americans are facing a lot of hate and discrimination, especially after Sept. 11 and most importantly after the election of Donald Trump. Rashida Tlaib's victory speaks volumes of our state and the people in our state. It's a slap on the right cheek of Mr. Trump.
>
> *Burke, Ferretti, and Noble 2018*

What some constituents liked about Tlaib was her ability not to compromise who she was in running for political office and still be accepted by the voters. One supporter, Amer Zahr, a comedian, activist and adjunct professor of law at the University of Detroit Mercy stated:

> That's how monumental this is. She is an Arab American, Palestinian-American who can win while fully embracing her identity and not having to backtrack on her beliefs. It shows she can be genuine to her culture and values and still win a seat in Congress.
>
> *Burke, Ferretti, and Noble 2018*

This statement illustrates the psychological attachment Arab Americans have with Tlaib and her candidacy. The group attachment to Tlaib also led Arab Americans to contribute to her campaign. Ghassan M. Saed, an assistant professor in obstetrics and gynecology at Wayne State University told the Detroit News that he donated to her campaign because he wanted Tlaib to be the first female Arab Muslim in Congress: "I like to support females, minorities and different religions," Saed said. "We have to be representing everybody in this society. I think it's very important because it will kill the Islamophobia that is simply going on. Our voice will be heard" (Burke, Ferretti, and Noble 2018). Again, this strengthens Simien's theory that historic firsts like Rashida Tlaib can symbolically empower Arab Americans, Muslims, and women. The rest of the chapter will examine whether shared history and pride for historic firsts' candidacy is reciprocated by the candidate when they take elected office. Do Arab Americans and Muslims receive greater substantive representation of their interests?

Arab Americans, Muslims, Group Consciousness, and Political Representation

Even though Tlaib did not explicitly focus on the symbolic importance of her candidacy during the campaign, she discussed it much more after the election.

After her victory in the Democratic primary, she said she would represent all these groups, "I'm going to be a woman, a mom, a Muslimah, a Palestinian, an Arab and so many of these other layers of these identities depending on who I'm talking to and what they want to identify me as" (Zhou 2018). Symbolic empowerment was important to her Arab American and Muslim constituents, but would we expect Tlaib to feel that sense of attachment and commitment when she goes to Congress, primarily because legislators are motivated by their desire to be reelected (Mayhew 1974). They may have other goals, such as making good public policy and providing good constituency service, but they spend the bulk of this time on electoral goals (Fenno 1973). Thus, constituents in their district should have a significant impact of what issues legislators decide to represent more than their descriptive characteristics.

Tlaib represents a majority Black district that includes Detroit. Blacks are usually cohesive in their policy preferences and their voting. Although Arab Americans represent a larger proportion of the district than the state of Michigan, they represent a small portion of the district voters. Existing research is unclear on whether Arab Americans have policy preferences that are different from whites or vote differently from whites. Most public opinion surveys do not provide this information by ethnicity because Arab Americans are classified as white. Similar challenges exist in trying to obtain policy preferences for Muslims. Also, Muslims are a diverse group in the United States that includes people of Middle Eastern and African descent. Most of the people in Tlaib's district are Christian and not Muslim, thus her attentiveness to issues important to Muslims is unclear. Tlaib also represents the third poorest district in the nation, where the median family income is $34,971. To the extent she will advocate for policies to help the poor is not certain. Miler (2018) found that most legislators in poor districts were less likely to represent the interests of the poor. Finally, some scholars conclude that race or ethnicity of the candidate does not necessarily lead to the substantive representation of minority interests in Congress (Guinier 1994: Hero and Tolbert 1995; Overby and Cosgrove 1996; Swain 1993). They found that once the legislators' political party is accounted for then race or ethnicity has little impact on their behavior. Why would we expect Tlaib to behave differently from most legislators? The next section will explore whether ethnic and/or religious background can affect her ability to advocate for these groups.

With the factors mentioned above that constrain legislators' behavior, why would we expect her to substantively represent the groups that she symbolically empowered? The overwhelming majority of empirical and theoretical studies regarding the political representation of minorities demonstrate that race, ethnicity, and gender of legislators lead to effective substantive representation of these marginalized groups in legislatures. Specifically, Black and Latino legislators were more likely to sponsor and vote on legislation favored by Black and Latino constituents (Bratton and Haynie 1999; Brown 2014; Casellas 2011; Canon 1999; Grose 2011; Lublin 1997; Rouse 2013; Tate 2003; Tyson 2016; Wallace 2014;

Whitby 1997); participate in committee mark-ups to benefit minorities (Gamble 2007; Hall 1996); and engage in oversight of federal agencies that oversee the implementation of policies important to minorities (Minta 2011; Minta 2009).

Although legislators are motivated by the desire to be re-elected to office, for racial or ethnic minorities there are non-strategic factors that motivate their legislative activity. Much has been written about racial or ethnic group consciousness or a commitment to engage in actions that will advance the interests of the group due to a shared history of discrimination, but not much has been written on religious group consciousness. Muslims are from various racial, ethnic, and cultural backgrounds in the United States. Despite their heterogeneity, there is an expectation that they will possess ethnic and religious group consciousness because of the threats and discrimination they receive because of their religion. Radical Islamists were responsible for the September 11 terrorist attacks in New York and Washington, D.C., but many Americans have developed a distrust of Muslims. Tlaib is also of Palestinian descent and is familiar with the struggle by Palestinians to gain representation in the West Bank. Tlaib understands the importance of providing a voice to issues not typically heard in Congress. In addition to her unique perspective, Tlaib has the lived experience of being of Palestinian descent in the United States and provides situated knowledge that non-descriptive representatives cannot. Her intersectional identity as a child of Palestinian immigrants, a Muslim, and a woman helps shape how she represents constituents in her district (Brown 2014; Simien 2015). In 2019, she discussed this point during at keynote address at a Muslim Public Affairs Convention (MPAC):

> I want them to see that the strength of me being a Palestinian American, a woman who is the child of immigrants, the eldest of 14, that I wasn't going to back down, I wasn't going to sell out, because I have seen the pain in my parents' eyes every time they felt like they were being sold out.
>
> *Twair 2020*

On the importance of winning and her connection to the Arab American community:

> When you see a Palestinian person with your name and faith succeed, it shows [the government] can ban us from coming into the country but not from getting elected. Showing people, it can be done would be a victory to my family.
>
> *Venkataramanan 2018*

Some scholars found religious group consciousness for Muslims can be enhanced by attending mosques. Jamal (2005) found that Arab Muslims participation in mosque is related to direct mobilization and an increase in group consciousness and civic skills. Arab Americans and Black Muslims who go to mosque are likely to know someone who discriminated against them because of their religious beliefs. Tlaib's background will lead her to represent the interests of Blacks and Latinos who also have experienced racial/ethnic discrimination in the United States. At MPAC she stated: "Every time I see some sort of economic oppression against my Black brothers and sisters, the 'othering' and dehumanization of my immigrant neighbors, it reminds me of what my family continues to go through in Palestine" (Twair 2020). CAIR, a national advocacy group, plays a large role in mobilizing voters who are Muslim and recruiting candidates to run. Like many legislators, Tlaib is a member of legislative caucuses. Caucus membership can provide the informational resources and support necessary for legislators to engage in advocacy. She is a member of caucuses such as the Democratic Women's Caucus and the Congressional Progressive Caucus. A shared history of discrimination experienced by Arab Americans and Muslims should motivate Tlaib to represent the interests of these groups. Additionally, her membership in progressive caucuses and being a Democratic Socialist should motivate her to represent the interests of poor and working families. The following sections will examine whether her ethnic and religious group identification will lead to effective representation of women and minority interests in substantive activities such as roll call voting, bills sponsorship, and oversight of federal agencies.

From Symbols to the Substantive Representation of Arab Americans and Muslims

Although Tlaib's presence in Congress provides important symbolic value to Arab Americans and Muslims, she actively works to ensure that existing laws and policies are adequately protecting and including these groups. Adhering to her campaign promise, Tlaib introduced a resolution in March 2019 calling for the impeachment of President Donald Trump (see Table 5.5 for details). House Speaker Nancy Pelosi argued that focusing on impeachment would distract Democrats from issues necessary to help the party win such as healthcare and the economy. As a result, the resolution garnered only 17 co-sponsors and did not receive much support from party leadership or rank and file members. Responding to the mounting pressure from the Democratic base, House leadership eventually agreed to proceed with impeachment against Trump. He was impeached in 2020 with Tlaib voting in favor of his impeachment. Although the Senate voted not to remove the president, the movement that sent Tlaib to Congress accomplished its goal. Impeachment animated her campaign, but it has not defined her legislative agenda.

In 2019, the House Oversight and Reform Committee held several hearings that focused on ways to combat white supremacy and discrimination in the United States. She provides an account of the discrimination that Muslims face in the United States, encourages the agency to do more to identify hate groups,

TABLE 5.5 Selected Bills and Resolutions Introduced by Tlaib, 116th Congress (2019–2020)

Bills or Resolutions Introduced	Description/Summary
H.Res.257—Inquiring whether the House of Representatives should impeach Donald John Trump, President of the United States of America.	This resolution directs the House Committee on the Judiciary to inquire whether the House of Representatives should impeach President Donald John Trump.
H.R.6553—Automatic Boost to Communities Act	To direct the Secretary of the Treasury to establish the Boost Communities Program to provide monthly payments to America's consumers during the COVID–19 emergency to recover from the emergency, and for other purposes.
H.R.6552—Emergency Water is a Human Right Act	To prohibit water shutoffs during the COVID–19 emergency period, provide drinking and wastewater assistance to households, and for other purposes.
H.R.1675—Petroleum Coke Transparency and Public Health Protection Act	To require a study on the public health and environmental impacts of the production, transportation, storage, and use of petroleum coke, and for other purposes.
H.Res.948—Expressing support for the recognition of April as Arab American Heritage Month and celebrating the heritage and culture of Arab Americans in the United States.	This resolution supports the designation of an Arab American Heritage Month.
H.R.1756—Preventing Credit Score Discrimination in Auto Insurance Act	This bill prohibits the use of a credit report, a credit score, or other consumer information in determining auto insurance coverage or rates.

Source: Congress.gov, Library of Congress.

and questions the FBI on what they are doing to address hate crimes against Muslims,

> My understanding is that the remaining 80 percent of the FBI's pending counterterrorism cases would be characterized as the international, you called them H—I hate these labels, by the way, it drives me—as a Muslim, like I just hate them because it automatically makes me feel like people are

targeting those of different faiths and colors and so forth. But called HVE cases.

U.S. Congress, Subcommittee on Confronting White Supremacy 2019a

Her intersectional identities as a Muslim woman plays a role in leading her to attend and participate in committee deliberations. She also recounts how she has been subject to discrimination during her time in Congress.

> So, I want to give an example. So, I've been in office for about six months. And when you get something like this: "Attention Congresswoman Alexandria Ocasio-Cortez and ragheads Rashida Tlaib and Ilhan Omar, I was totally excited and pleased when I heard about 49 Muslims were killed and many—many more were wounded in New Zealand. This is a great start. Let's hope and pray that it continues here in the good old USA. The only good Muslim is a dead one."
>
> *U.S. Congress, Subcommittee on Confronting White Supremacy 2019b*

Another important issue that came before the Congress is whether Arab Americans be included as a separate category in the U.S. Census. In the United States, Arab Americans are not a separate racial category and are considered white. Tlaib argues that the classification ignores that most Arab Americans are not white but are people of color. She attends an oversight hearing devoted to the Census. She details past efforts by advocacy groups to get a separate ethnic category on the Census to fairly represent Arab Americans and North Africans. In a 2019 hearing held by the Committee on Oversight and Reform, she questioned Secretary of Commerce Wilbur L. Ross, Jr., about when or if the Middle Eastern and North African (MENA) ethnicity question would be added to the 2020 Census. She argues the MENA are not white and that category would adequately affect people from this part of the world. Ross states that he will investigate it more (U.S. Congress 2019, Committee on Oversight and Reform, with Census Bureau Director). One year later, the committee conducted another hearing, and Tlaib was not pleased that the Census Bureau did not include the MENA category on the Census. In comments directed at Census Bureau Director, Dr. Steven Dillingham, Tlaib explains the logic on why it is important to have the designation included on the census questionnaire:

> That is why the community pushed to add the category of MENA, and they did it right. They went through the process, and they got it approved. And this Administration decided to ignore them and to make them invisible again, right? That is what you are doing. You are making us invisible. No, the continued absence of this ethnic category contributes to erasing us, our living, working—we all live and work and raise our families here. I truly believe this issue needs to be addressed, and we need your leadership to push back against this current Administration's lack of wanting to see people like me being represented on an official government Federal form, that decides

funding, decides how they are going to treat us, how they are going to approach health research, language assistance, all those kinds of things.

U.S. Congress, Committee on Oversight and Reform 2020,
with Census Bureau Director

To emphasize her point she asks the director, "Dr. Dillingham, do I look white to you?" (U.S. Congress, Committee on Oversight and Reform 2020, with Census Bureau Director).

Despite Tlaib's Middle Eastern heritage and constituents of Arab descent, she does not serve on a committee that addresses international issues. In a majority Black district with a sizable but relatively small Arab population, many of her district constituents would not consider the Israeli-Palestinian conflict a top issue. Despite the public controversy regarding the Israeli prime minister, Ben Netanyahu, banning her and fellow "Squad" members from traveling to the country, Tlaib has managed to stay out of the spotlight and does not pick fights with the powerful Israeli lobby. Even in her House floor speeches, she does not mention those issues. This is in marked contrast to Rep. Omar (D-MN) who has had several disagreements with the American Israel Public Affair Committee.

The advocacy of Tlaib in these hearings demonstrate that Tlaib's victory translates into substantive advocacy on issues of importance to Arab Americans and Muslims. No other legislator at the congressional hearings addresses these issues as it relates to Arab Americans and Muslims. She provides a voice to groups that are not normally represented in the legislative arena.

Civil Rights for Blacks and Latinos

Tlaib directs her attention on broadly reaching economic justice issues. Race, class, and other issues are included, but racial issues are not highlighted in her bills. She differs from Conyers in that she does not necessarily introduce explicitly racial or ethnic bills. Tlaib mentions equity and social justice but does not prominently highlight race as part of her legislative agenda. For years, Conyers sponsored and championed racial justice issues. He supported and sponsored the reparation bills and criminal justice reforms. He championed the cause of Black farmers even though there weren't any farmers in his district. Tlaib is a freshman in a very competitive primary. Her strategy is different from Steve Cohen, the other non–Black who represents a majority Black district, who has championed explicitly racial issues such as reparations, criminal justice, or class issues. He serves on House Judiciary while Tlaib serves on House Financial Services and Oversight and Reform. So, maybe the committee jurisdiction may play a big role on where and what she decides to focus on. Tlaib introduced a bill to prevent consumer credit reports from determining auto insurance rates, primarily because credit scores can be based on other factors such as where a person lives, and not just their history of repayment. Most of the bills introduced by legislators do not become law, but they do provide an important view on the issues that are important to members and their constituents. Even though the Democrats are in the majority in the House, they do not control the Senate or the presidency, so the likelihood of getting any of the bills she sponsored passed into law are very low.

In 2019, Tlaib's highly controversial vote against the Democratic Party supported $4.6 billion border aid package obscures the degree of support she has for Latino issues. She voted against the package because she believed that the bill did not do enough to help fix the problems with immigration and the border. Like most freshmen, she does not hold a leadership position on the full committee or a subcommittee, so they used the power of oversight to help draw attention to the issue. Tlaib and Squad members asked Rep. Elijah Cummings, chair of the Oversight and Reform Committee, whether they could go to the U.S.–Mexico border to examine how immigrant children were treated. The committee held a hearing in which Tlaib testified to report on the issues that they found at the detention system in Texas. She detailed the inhumane conditions immigrants face at the southern border. She is concerned about the CBP ideology that agents shouldn't tell on each other. She worries about the long-term effects on children who are being kept in cages at the border. Tlaib recommends a program that allows asylum-seekers to reside in the community instead of in detention centers. Tlaib notes that during the 80's, when there was even more immigration at the southern border, detention was rare for asylum-seekers (U.S. Congress, Subcommittee on Civil Rights and Civil Liberties 2019). Their experience at the border helped inform their perspective and thus they could not support a bill that did not go far enough to solve the problems. When criticized about her vote Tlaib said: "I will not vote for something that is broken and deteriorated and is inhumane. That is a choice I make and a conscious choice, and I can tell you my district supports me 100 percent" (Burke 2019).

Women's Issues

Tlaib's rise to power came in part due to the backlash by women to Trump's presidency. She is a member of the Democratic Women's Caucus and devotes time to advocating for issues that affect women and children. She draws upon her lived experience as a mother as she expressed her concern of the manufacturing of nicotine products to attract young people. In a hearing relating to the federal response to the increasing use of electronic cigarettes by children she states,

> "Sorry. I am a mom of two young boys, and I am just trying to make sure that we resolve this before, not only juice boxes, but we are going to have candy or suckers out there with this stuff"
>
> *U.S. Congress, Subcommittee on Economic and Consumer Policy 2019*

Specifically, telling the FDA director that manufacturing these products to appeal to children is unacceptable. In this hearing and many others, Tlaib uses her experience as a mother to motivate her concern for better public policies to address issues that impact children.

She also addresses how people with intersectional identities such as race and gender are affected differently from others. She discusses access to reproductive healthcare in relation to the infant mortality rate and maternal mortality rate, especially for Black and other women of color.

> Dr. McNicholas, you know, Missouri was one of the highest rates—has the highest rates of maternal mortality in the country, and that continues to rise, especially among women of color. In fact, Black women in Missouri are three times more likely to die from pregnancy complications than other women.
>
> *U.S. Congress, Subcommittee on Examining State Efforts to*
> *Undermine Access to Reproductive Health Care 2019*

She is concerned about the lack of access to maternal care in rural areas, especially in Missouri, where she states the Director of the Department of Public Health spends more time trying to shut down Planned Parenthood than worrying about maternal health. Her experience as a Palestinian American and Muslim mother helps provide context for advocacy efforts on behalf of minority women and their children.

Environmental Justice and Fighting Corporate Greed

Economic justice and the environment are not the traditional issues pushed by legislators representing majority Black districts. In a survey of Black public opinion, the environment rates near the bottom. Tlaib's message related directly to environmental justice issues that she has long championed from her years in the state legislature. She fought corporations that dumped waste in poor and minority communities. In Congress, she introduced the environmental justice bill to take on polluters in her district. Tlaib argues that corporate greed or the willingness of corporations to put profits over the health and safety of consumers, should be addressed by Congress. In a hearing focused on harmful chemicals in consumer products such as baby powder and make-up for teenage girls, Tlaib speaks to how the problem affects working class families and people of color:

> I think people are not realizing corporate greed is a type of cancer in our democracy right now, and it is true. Just last week, the Food and Drug Administration issued a safety alert confirming that asbestos was found in make-up product samples from stores like Claire's and Justice, which are the stores that my residents go to, working folks, working families. They do not

go to the bourgeois Macy's counter. I am being serious. These are targeting working-class people, companies that manufacture and sell these make-up products to young girls, many of them of color.

U.S. Congress, Subcommittee on Economic and Consumer Policy 2019

Tlaib, along with other Democrats on the committee, wants Congress to strengthen the power of the FDA to recall personal care products and cosmetics. Under current law, the FDA does not have the power to make companies like Claire's recall harmful products. The agency can only make recommendations or issue safety alerts. She wants to put the harmful products on her website to warn young girls but wants Congress to pass the legislation to save people's lives.

Tlaib's focus on environmental justice brings a new dimension to minority representation. Although minorities are more likely to be a victim of toxic pollution or live near a landfill, Black and Latinos usually list environmental concerns as a low priority. Even though it is not a traditional civil rights issue or highly salient to the minority community, she understands the importance and the impact pollution has on minority health. As a Michigan state legislator, she devoted significant time advocating for the state to hold corporations accountable for polluting air and water. She continues this advocacy in the U.S. Congress. For instance, she introduced a bill to require the Department of Health and Human Services to study the impact that petroleum coke usage had on people's health and the environment. The Environmental Protection Agency would make rules based on the study to help protect citizens' health and the environment. She is the vice-chair of the subcommittee on Environment for House Oversight and Reform. Working with subcommittee and full committee chair, she requested that a hearing be held in Michigan about the environmental concerns affecting her district and Michigan in general. The hearing focused on the inequities in air and water quality in Michigan. Specifically, big corporations such as Marathon and its release of chemicals into the air. Tlaib states:

I am going to focus today on two truths: we have a right to breathe clean air, and water is a human right. I have been in this fight for environmental justice for a long time. Growing up, I did think that smell was normal from industrial pollution. Entire generations grow up in sacrifice zones where our air and water are polluted by wealthy corporations for profit, and we are expected to accept that.

U.S. Congress, Subcommittee on Environmental Justice 2019

Also, Tlaib planned to introduce a bill to combat environmental racism. She wants to go after corporate and government polluters.

[The Justice For All Civil Rights Act] is not just going to be about corporate polluters but also our own government, which now is not creating a pathway to affordable water, that you are seeing a lot of implementation at all levels of government where our communities, especially communities of color and low-income communities, and many parts of my Wayne County community are not only African American but they are also very, very poor white, Latino communities that are literally not getting access to the same protections that other communities have.

U.S. Congress, Subcommittee on Environmental Justice 2019

Conclusion

In 2019, *The Arab American News* named Rashida Tlaib as their "2019 Person of the Year" (Myer 2019). Her victory symbolized to Arab Americans, Muslims, and women that they are important part of the fabric of America. In a very close electoral race, her ability to get these traditional overlooked groups involved in the electoral process played a role in helping her win a very competitive electoral competition in a majority Black district. Tlaib's victory can be seen as part of a combination of multiple social movements. She was part of the 2016 women's movement that openly rejected President Donald Trump's past treatment of women. Part of her campaign was to provide a voice to women. She was also part of the movement to reject the anti-Arab and Muslim sentiment coming from conservatives and the Trump administration. Lastly, she is a Democratic Socialist and is part of the larger movement such as the Occupy Wall Street and other progressives that propelled Bernie Sanders as a major presidential candidate and Ilhan Omar and Alexandria Ocasio Cortez to Congress. Thus, it is not surprising Tlaib is a big supporter of Bernie Sanders and liberal policies. All these factors help explain why Tlaib engages in activities that are representative of the district beyond standard strategic explanations.

She is a fierce advocate for all groups in her district especially Arab Americans, women, and Black and brown people. She has sponsored legislation that demonstrates her commitment to a progressive social agenda. Tlaib campaigned on civil rights and economic and social justice issues. Her record in Congress demonstrates that she effectively represents these positions in her lawmaking activities, bill introductions and the oversight of federal agencies. She represents women's issues, racial and ethnic minority issues, and environmental justice. She engages in oversight at hearings and calls federal agencies to task for not representing these issues. Minta (2011) found that Congress spends most of its time overseeing the implementation of existing federal laws and regulations and not necessarily passing new laws. Tlaib also introduces bills to change laws and the nature of the bills fit her style of representation where she represents working class families.

With Tlaib's public disputes with President Trump and unofficial membership in the "Squad," she will have to guard against accusations that she does not pay adequate attention to the needs of the district. In 2020, Detroit City Council President, Brenda Jones challenged Tlaib again for the Democratic Party nomination. Jones argued that Tlaib spent too much time focusing on national issues and not the needs of the district such as addressing poverty and unemployment. This time Jones was the only challenger and was endorsed by her 2018 competitors, Coleman Young, Jr., Ian Conyers, and Bill Weld. With this united front, many in popular media wrote that Tlaib was the most vulnerable of the "Squad" members because of unapologetic style and progressive politics (Burnett 2020). In August 2020, Tlaib once again emerged victorious over Jones in the Democratic primary, winning in a landslide (State of Michigan 2020). The victory solidifies that her historic victory in 2018 was not a fluke of a crowded primary. She is a skilled campaigner who not only symbolically empowers women, Arab Americans, and Muslims, but she substantively represents the interests of all the constituents in her district, especially marginalized groups.

References

Bratton, Kathleen A., and Kerry L. Haynie. 1999. "Agenda Setting and Legislative Success in State Legislatures: The Effects of Gender and Race." *Journal of Politics* 61: 658–679.

Brennan, David. 2019. "Rashida Tlaib Inspires Thousands of Palestinians to Pose in Traditional Dress." *Newsweek*, January 4, 2019. www.newsweek.com/rashida-tlaib-traditional-dress-palestinian-twitter-swearing-thobe-1279369

Brown, Nadia. E. 2014. *Sisters in the Statehouse: Black Women & Legislative Decision making.* New York: Oxford University Press.

Burnett, Sara. 2020. "'Squad Member' Tlaib May Be Vulnerable in Tough Primary." *AP News*, July 23, 2020.

Burke, Melissa Nann. 2018. "Clerk Tosses Conyers III From Congress Ballot." *Detroit News*, May 21, 2018.

Burke, Melissa Nann, Christine Ferretti, and Breana Noble. 2018. "Tlaib: Brother's golf cart helped her become first Muslim woman elected to Congress." *The Detroit News*, August 8, 2018.

Burke, Melissa Nann. 2019. "Tlaib Hits Back at Pelosi Over Border Bill Criticism." *The Detroit News*, July 8, 2019.

Canon, David T. 1999. *Race, Redistricting, and Representation: The Unintended Consequences of Black Majority Districts.* Chicago: University of Chicago Press.

Casellas, Jason P. 2011. *Latino Representation in State Houses and Congress.* New York: Cambridge University Press.

Center for Responsive Politics, Politicians and Elections, Congressional Races, Michigan, 2018. Editor. "City Council president Brenda Jones makes bid for Congress." *Michigan Chronicle*, June 27, 2018.

Fenno, Richard F., Jr. 1973. *Congressmen in Committees.* Boston: Little, Brown and Company.

Gamble, Katrina L. 2007. "Black Political Representation: An Examination of Legislative Activity Within U.S. House Committees." *Legislative Studies Quarterly* 32: 421–447.

Grose, Christian. 2011. *Congress in Black and White: Race and Representation in Washington and at Home*. New York: Cambridge University Press.

Guinier, Lani. 1994. *The Tyranny of the Majority: Fundamental Fairness in Representative Democracy*. New York: The Free Press.

Hagen, Lisa. 2018. "Dem hoping to replace Conyers pushes Trump impeachment." *The Hill*, April 4. https://thehill.com/homenews/campaign/381525-dem-hoping-to-replace-conyers-pushes-trump-impeachment

Hall, Richard L. 1996. *Participation in Congress*. New Haven: Yale University Press.

Hero, Rodney E., and Caroline J. Tolbert. 1995. "Latinos and Substantive Representation in the U.S. House of Representatives: Direct, Indirect, or Nonexistent?" *American Journal of Political Science* 39: 640–652.

Jamal, Amaney. 2005. "The Political Participation and Engagement of Muslim Americans: Mosque Involvement and Group Consciousness." *American Politics Research* 33: 521–544.

Lublin, David. 1997. *The Paradox of Representation: Racial Gerrymandering and Minority Interests in Congress*. Princeton, NJ: Princeton University Press.

Mayhew, David R. 1974. *Congress: The Electoral Connection*. New Haven, CT: Yale University Press.

Miler, Kristina C. 2018. *Poor Representation: Congress and the Politics of Poverty in the United States*. New York: Cambridge University.

Minta, Michael D. 2009. "Legislative Oversight and the Substantive Representation of Black and Latino Interests in Congress." *Legislative Studies Quarterly* 34: 193–218.

Minta, Michael D. 2011. *Oversight: Representing Black and Latino Interests in Congress*. Princeton, NJ: Princeton University Press. Myer, Nick. 2019. "The Arab American News Names Congresswoman Rashida Tlaib '2019 Person of the Year.'" *The Arab American News*, March 27, 2019.

Overby, L. Marvin and Kenneth M. Cosgrove. 1996. "Unintended Consequences? Racial Redistricting and the Representation of Minority Interests." *Journal of Politics* 58: 540–550.

Rouse, Stella M. 2013. *Latinos in the Legislative Process: Interests and Influence*. New York: Cambridge University Press.

Rupar, Aaron. 2019. "New Congress member creates stir by saying of Trump: 'We're going to impeach this motherfucker!'" *Vox*, January 4. www.vox.com/policy-and-politics/2019/1/4/18168157/rashida-tlaib-trump-impeachment-motherfucker

Simien, Evelyn M. 2015. *Historic Firsts: How Symbolic Empowerment Changes U.S. Politics*. New York: Oxford University Press.

State of Michigan, Department of State. 2018. Michigan Election Results, General, November 6, 2018. https://mielections.us/election/results/2018GEN_CENR.html

State of Michigan, Department of State. 2020. Michigan Election Results, Primary, August 4, 2020. https://mielections.us/election/results/2020PRI_CENR.html

Suchyta, Sue. 2019. "Rashida Tlaib: An Arab American woman's rise to Congress." *Press & Guide*, April 18, 2019. www.pressandguide.com/news/rashida-tlaib-an-arab-american-woman-s-rise-to-congress/article_b5ac5c24-6211-11e9-addd-cb9dffac23c3.html

Swain, Carol M. 1993. *Black Faces, Black Interests: The Representation of African Americans in Congress*. Cambridge: Harvard University Press.

Tate, Katherine. 2003. *Black Faces in the Mirror: African Americans and Their Representatives in the U.S. Congress*. Princeton, NJ: Princeton University Press.

Twair, Samir. 2020. "Rep. Rashida Tlaib Highlights MPAC Convention." *Washington Report on Middle East Affairs* 39(1): 54–55.

Tyson, Vanessa C. 2016. *Twists of Fate: Multiracial Coalitions and Minority Representation in the U.S. House of Representatives*. New York: Oxford University Press.

U.S. Congress, Committee on Oversight and Reform. 2019. 116th Congress, March 14. (Statement of Rashida Tlaib, U.S. House Representative from Michigan, with Census Bureau Director).

U.S. Congress, Committee on Oversight and Reform, Subcommittee on Civil Rights and Civil Liberties. 2019. 116th Congress, July 10. (Statement of Rashida Tlaib, U.S. House Representative from Michigan).

U.S. Congress, Committee on Oversight and Reform, Subcommittee on Confronting White Supremacy. 2019a. 116th Congress, May 15. (Statement of Rashida Tlaib, U.S. House Representative from Michigan).

U.S. Congress, Committee on Oversight and Reform, Subcommittee on Confronting White Supremacy. 2019b. 116th Congress, June 14. (Statement of Rashida Tlaib, U.S. House Representative from Michigan).

U.S. Congress, Committee on Oversight and Reform, Subcommittee on Economic and Consumer Policy. 116th Congress, 2019, December 4. (Statement of Rashida Tlaib, U.S. House Representative from Michigan).

U.S. Congress, Committee on Oversight and Reform, Subcommittee on Environmental Justice: Exploring Inequities in Air and Water Quality, 2019. 116th Congress, September 16. (Statement of Rashida Tlaib, U.S. House Representation from Michigan).

U.S. Congress, Committee on Oversight and Reform, Subcommittee on Examining State Efforts to Undermine Access to Reproductive Health Care. 2019. 116th Congress, November 14. (Statement of Rashida Tlaib, U.S. House Representative from Michigan).

U.S. Congress, Committee on Oversight and Reform. 116th Congress, 2020. Second Session, February 12. (Statement of Rashida Tlaib, U.S. House Representative from Michigan, with Census Bureau Director).

Venkataramanan, Meena. "Muslim-American Women Hope to Make History in Midterm Elections." ABC News, August 5, 2018.

Wallace, Sophia J. 2014. "Representing Latinos: Examining Descriptive and Substantive Representation in Congress." *Political Research Quarterly* 67: 917–929.

Whitby, Kenny J. 1997. *The Color of Representation: Congressional Behavior and Black Interests*. Ann Arbor: University of Michigan Press.

Zhou, Li. 2018. "Rashida Tlaib is set to be one of the first Muslim American women in Congress," *Vox*, August 8. www.vox.com/policy-and-politics/2018/8/8/17663896/rashida-tlaib-muslim-american-woman-congress-michigan.

6

MAYOR LONDON BREED AND THE LIMITS OF GOVERNING WHILE BLACK AND FEMALE IN SAN FRANCISCO

Chelsea N. Jones, Crystal Robertson, and Lorrie Frasure

London Breed won a hotly contested mayoral election to become the first Black female mayor in San Francisco's 200-year history. Given the city's majority white and Asian populations, sparse Black population of about 5 percent, and storied history of LGBTQ activism, Breed's historic victory over an Asian woman and an openly gay white male, creates a lens through which to examine the role that descriptive representation, symbolic empowerment, and deracialization play in determining a candidate's electoral strategy and success. Using a case study approach, we examine Breed's electoral campaign success and the first two years of governing, including through the rising Black Lives Matter protests in response to racialized police violence.

London Breed's campaign is a unique example of how the theories of symbolic empowerment and deracialization can combine to produce historic electoral success. To Black voters in San Francisco, Breed's symbolism as the potential first Black, female mayor was reflective of the city's ability to overcome its history of systemic racism and oppressive housing; economic and criminal justice policies that ravaged its last remaining Black neighborhood. Breed's identification with this community signaled to Black voters that she represented their interests which motivated them to overwhelmingly support her candidacy as she became an archetype of hope for a despairing people.

Though Breed found success in inspiring the Black community, San Francisco's diversity required a broader appeal to a multi-racial coalition. Breed's campaign could be viewed by many as deracialized because she spoke about racial minority issues in universal terms, and chose policy items—schools, health care, immigration, LGBTQ rights, and broad economic approaches—that did not directly target the African-American population, even if the issues might have beneficial impact to the group. Critics might charge that she avoided a racialized campaign for

DOI: 10.4324/9781003213925-6

political reasons, while supporters argue that this was a pragmatic approach toward success at the ballot box. Ultimately, this strategy did not sway Black voter turnout, as members of San Francisco's Black community casted their vote for Breed, with high hopes that she would best represent their interests.

In this chapter, we will investigate the ways in which London Breed's campaign evoked themes of hope and restoration to capture the votes of Black San Franciscans, while also employing deracialization techniques to capture a diverse group of non-Black voters. To do so, we analyze descriptive statistics connecting San Franciscan's demographics and issue orientations to the field of San Francisco mayoral candidates.[1] We utilize the reporting of election survey data from 2018 that captures San Franciscans attitudes toward the candidates in the months leading up to the mayoral election. Our case study analyzes Breed's campaign and the images, rhetoric and strategies that worked together to reinvigorate Black voters and create a multiracial coalition. The latter part of this chapter underscores the long-standing debate over the extent to which a deracialized electoral strategy can be translated into a governance strategy (Perry 1991), particularly for women of color elected officials. Considering the resurgence of Black Lives Matter protests (simultaneous to the time of this research), the case study also illustrates the strategies employed in Breed's current governance; assessing the methods used to address the exasperation of existing racial disparities and racial injustices permeating San Francisco, before these events. The next section outlines the material conditions and history of inequity which led Black voters to perceiving London Breed's candidacy as a pivotal point in the city's history. Then, we move on to the case study of London Breed's campaign and analysis of her governance since elected in 2018.

An Unexpected Ascension to Leadership

London Breed's term as Mayor began in 2017, after the tragic and unexpected death of Mayor Ed Lee (Chappel and Gonzales 2017). As the current president of the San Francisco board of supervisors, Breed was thrust into the position to carry the mantle forward and reassure San Franciscans that the city would continue to be run well. Breed's tenure as interim Mayor was cut short however, when her fellow members of the Board of Supervisors argued that Breed wielded too much power as both president of the board and acting Mayor. Other officials argued that Breed's position as interim Mayor would sway the upcoming election, unduly providing her with an incumbency advantage (Knight 2018b).

Only one month after taking her position, Breed was voted out of the Mayor's office and replaced by a wealthy, white male supervisor, Mark Farrell, who was not in the race. These actions were seen by the public as a concerted effort from Breed's then colleagues and potential competitors to subvert her growing influence. Jane Kim, a fellow supervisor, and mayoral candidate was a leader of that charge (Boney 2018).

Though the goal may have been to obstruct Breed's mayoral campaign, it led Black voters to double down on their commitment to her in response to what they saw as a racially motivated attack. Breed's ascension to the mayorship mirrored that of the only other woman mayor, Diane Fienstein, who had become mayor after the assassination of George Moscone in 1978 (A & E 2018). However, Feinstein's position was not challenged, which led Black voters to acknowledge the only difference between the two situations—Breed's blackness (Levy-Wolins 2018). Voters saw her ousting as another instance of non-Black, wealthy political elites undermining the hard-earned success and accomplishments of Black women. In summarizing the turn of events, journalist Joe Eskenazi describes it this way:

> In short, the left-leaning bloc of the city's legislative body, at this particular moment in American history, chose to unseat a Black woman who worked her way from public housing to City Hall and replace her with a well-off white venture capitalist who graduated from St. Ignatius High and lives in the Marina.
>
> *Schneider and Boone 2018*

Initially, voters responded by flooding the city's board of supervisors meeting. Breed supporters, who were largely Black residents, spoke out against the other supervisors and pointed to racism as the deciding factor in the decision to have her removed (Levy-Wolins 2018). Many voters even booed and yelled "shame" when Farrell was granted her position (Press 2018). Amelia Ashley-Ward, owner of the San Francisco Sun-Reporter, San Francisco's trademark Black news publication, noted,

> London was ready, and she was qualified, but the way her colleagues on the Board of Supervisors bullied her and chose to push her out of her role as interim mayor truly energized the Black community to get behind her.
>
> *Boney 2018*

For these voters, supporting Breed became a more significant action; a form of resistance against a longstanding history of anti-Black policy decisions made by San Francisco Democrats.

Breed however, refused to acknowledge the racial underpinnings of this decision. When asked whether her removal was a result of racism, she noted "I don't want to dwell on that particular element because it has sadly brought out the worst in some people … what I'm trying to do … is bring out the best in people" (Shafer 2018). Whether Breed verbalized it or not, the messaging of this scandal reverberated through the Black community and increased the urgency of her election. For Black voters in San Francisco, the possibility of overcoming the legacy of racism in local politics presented itself in London Breed's candidacy.

To Be Black in the Bay: San Francisco's Troubled Racial History

Reverend Amos C. Brown is president of the San Francisco National Association for the Advancement of Colored People (NAACP) branch and pastor of San Francisco's landmark Black congregation, Third Baptist Church. His public comments often tell the true story of Black San Francisco, an institutionally and politically neglected community that has been left in the dust of rapid growth and innovation.

> I've been [a] pastor for 42 years now, and I've witnessed how so-called pro-gressive white liberals have played the Black community and have never been honest, straightforward participants in the welfare of Black people.
>
> *Press 2018*

Brown's church is in the heart of the Breed's childhood neighborhood, the Western Addition. The community was once a hub for Black life in San Francisco and referred to as "the Harlem of the West," but was ravaged by botched urban renewal and the retraction of city resources (Pepin and Watts 2006).

In the 1940s, San Francisco city planning officials promised a robust renewal that would include new and improved housing, schools, retail, and recreation, improving public health and financial security for community residents (Thompson 2016). Instead, large portions of housing units were demolished and never replaced, leaving Black residents trapped in blighted, redlined neighborhoods. Though the residents created community and culture amid rubble, this mismanagement natur-ally seeded feelings of government mistrust.

The Western Addition represents a broader story of political negligence that resonates with Black voters in San Francisco and beyond. Urban renewal destroyed property and increased poverty for Black people through the latter half of the 20th century. It opened the doors for Black residents to become the victims of crime, drug infestation and discriminatory policing. This is the imagery evoked at the mention of the Western Addition, and the context through which Breed's supporters find their greatest connection to her.

Breed's symbolic influence is not only in the historic nature of her candidacy, but in the closeness of her story to those of her voters. Throughout her cam-paign, Breed consistently presents herself as an underdog, reminding voters and her fellow candidates that she was raised by her grandmother in public housing, in the Western Addition. Breed relates to a common narrative among Black voters as someone who rose to political prominence from poverty, raised in a single parent, nontraditional household and personally impacted by the perils of familial drug abuse and an inequitable criminal justice system (Knight 2018a). Her identifica-tion with the Western Addition is a short cut for Black voters to see and feel that relation and project that experience onto her potential to become a successful lawmaker and advocate, as evidenced in the sentiments of April Spears, a Black restaurateur: "She comes from the same cloth that I do. I know that her will to better the inner-city community is high on her list" (Lapidus 2018).

Breed's campaign materials and rhetoric covertly indicate at her desire and ability to improve the conditions of her community. In her campaign profile video, Breed describes the Western Addition as an "amazing community with its challenges," and often notes that she's "… here to ensure that no one is left behind, like many of the people that I grew up in the Western Addition with" (Breed 2018b, Breed 2018c). These contemporary notions of abandonment are Breed's references to the drastic changes brought about by San Francisco's tech boom, that accelerated the city's financial gains while disparaging Black and low-income residents (Fuller 2016).

While many politicians (including Breed) are critiqued for being beholden to the tech industry, Breed's connection to the Western Addition and experience in poverty positions her as empathetic to San Franciscans on the struggling end of the city's growing wealth inequality. According to the Downsian theory of rational/economic voting, voters believe that the past (and their economic condition and a result of the past) is a window through which they can see the future and evaluate a candidate based on what benefits they've provided and/or will provide (Downs 1957). For Black residents of the Western Addition and San Francisco as a whole, the burden of wealth inequality, because of the policy decisions of previous Democratic leaders, created a pressing need for political revolution which Breed, and her non-traditional history, could provide.

A look into San Francisco's 2018 income statistics reveals how this wealth inequality has had a disparate impact on the Black community. According to data collected by the U.S. Census Bureau, the census tract representing the Western Addition reports a median household income of $22,500. However, this community is surrounded by census tracts where the median income ranges from $76,000 to $79,000 (U.S. Census Bureau, 2018). Black residents in San Francisco have a median income below the poverty line at $27,000, while white San Franciscans sit at about $89,000 (Fuller 2016).

In addition to exacerbating wealth inequality, San Francisco's dominance in the tech industry led to rampant gentrification which priced-out large fractions of the Black community. The Black population fell from over 13 percent in 1970 to about 5 percent by the 2018 election, leading to a dearth of Black life in the city (Garofoli 2018). According to the U.S. Census Bureau, no census tract in San Francisco boasts having greater than 53 percent Black population—not even the former epicenter of Black life, the Western Addition. The community is made up of about three census tracts that are 8, 26, and 32 percent Black (U.S. Census Bureau, 2018).

By the 2018 election, Black people in San Francisco had borne the brunt of rapid growth and development. For their community, income was low, jobs were scarce, friends and family members had been priced out of their homes, police violence had ravaged the streets and gentrification had stolen and replaced Black culture (Fuller 2016). Even the community church, Third Baptist Church, had experienced a consistent decline in worshippers, with about 150 attendees in a church built to accommodate over 1000. Suffice it to say, the Black community had lost its solid ground at the hands of the previous liberal politicians.

The dire predicament facing the Black community in San Francisco made London Breed's candidacy even more important. Breed's identity spoke to the concerns of these voters in ways she often did not verbalize. The symbolism of her not only identifying as a Black woman, but as one who had experienced poverty firsthand, was a drastic change of pace from San Francisco's legacy of wealthy white politicians. Breed's candidacy presented an opportunity for the Black community to rebuild with an advocate in the mayor (Fuller 2018). As Reverend Amos Brown puts it:

> We were fast becoming invisible people in this city … Maybe we can now stop this hemorrhaging.
>
> *Fuller 2016*

The structuring of Breed's campaign serves as evidence that she was aware of her positionality in the race. Breed weaved narratives of her upbringing to differentiate herself from the other candidates and implicitly be seen as an authentic member of the Black community. Breed often evokes memories of being raised by her grandmother, which is a central part of her personal story and reflects a common Black story of resiliency through reliance on extended family members (McCubbin et al. 1998). Her consistent mentions of her grandmother signal a familiar upbringing to Black voters, including that of attending church as a youth, sometimes unwillingly. Breed's campaign videos reflect on her grandmother as a "… strong, fierce woman" who went to church every Sunday, "and made [Breed and her siblings] go to church every Sunday" (Breed 2018b). To Black voters, London Breed's grandmother represents the archetype of the Black woman, one who is full of faith, strength and is generous even with very little. Naturally, these traits can be projected onto Breed as a candidate, allowing her to be seen as both empathetic, powerful, and influential to future generations.

The Woman Behind the Black Girl Magic: Symbolic Empowerment in SF

From the ardent support from her church to endorsements from key political and social figures in California, Breed empowered the Black community and its institutions to back her campaign. The clearest indication of that support is the election results. Reports note the 2018 San Francisco election was by far the closest and most competitive race the city of San Francisco has had for mayor since the 1995 election of the first Black mayor, Willie Brown. (Boney 2018). Data from FairVote California shows that many residents in the Western Addition supported Breed as their first-choice candidate (Hernandez 2018). As the Western Addition is home to one of San Francisco's largest Black populations in the city,

TABLE 6.1 Candidate Supporters by Race

	White	Black	Hispanic	Asian
Richie Greenberg	4	0	9	5
Mark Leno	7	3	19	18
Amy Weiss	1	11	0	1
Angelo Alioto	10	12	6	7
Jane Kim	14	1	9	18
Ellen Lee Zhou	1	2	0	4
Michelle Bravo	1	9	2	1
London Breed	17	48	23	16

Source: Survey USA 2018 Election Poll. Sample size (n):800 San Francisco adults.

this serves as an indirect indicator of Black support for Breed. The Survey USA data supports this inference. As shown is Table 6.1, Breed led her fellow candidates among Black supporters, with 48 percent of Black residents sampled ranking Breed as their first-choice candidate.

This support was also evident through the constant stream of headlines extolling London Breed in the Black Press, the San Francisco Bay View Newspaper, throughout her campaign and for months following her victory. In these articles they highlighted Breed's policies and plans for the city, shared information on registration and election details, and mobilized Black citizens to show up in support of the first Black woman who could be mayor of the city (Boney 2018). The reporters' uplifting of Breed helped ingratiate her to Black San Franciscans as trusted sources of information vouching for her character. With articles such as "White privilege ousts Black mayor" and "London Breed, you are my mayor too," the publication aimed to bolster Breed's standing in the Black community and develop a unified front of support for her candidacy (Jones 2018, Robertson 2018). Amelia Ashley-Ward, the owner of one Black San Francisco newspaper and former chairman of the National Newspaper Publishers Association Foundation describes her efforts to support Breed:

> She was on our front page every week for three months … We ran editorials, educated the entire community about the ranked-choice voting system, shared her platform, and encouraged people to become more familiar with who London Breed really was. As a result, more Black people got registered to vote, hosted fundraisers, held rallies and volunteered for her campaign. The Black Press and the Black community did everything possible to make sure London was elected and now she is.
>
> *Boney 2018*

Breed grew up in a Christian household where both she and her grandmother were part of the congregation at Third Baptist Church. Reverend Brown first knew Breed as a dedicated teenage church congregate participating in the youth council of the NAACP and friend to his children (KTVU 2018). Breed's dedication to serving her church from adolescence to her adult years resulted in ardent support from her congregation. Her fellow parishioners were some of the most vocal constituents to express outrage of at the Board of Supervisors' conspiracy to remove her from office. They publicly decried the removal as racially motivated and unethical, with her pastor Reverend Amos Brown explicitly calling the board racist for removing Breed from office (Fracassa 2019).

Reverend Brown was among the local civil rights leaders who accused the SF Board of Supervisors of supporting policies that contributed to income inequality and enforced punitive measures in health matters such as addiction and mental health concerns. In his defense of Breed, he made clear that he considers her a leading figure in progress for the city's African-American community. Rev Brown went on to say that "Opposing Breed was a tacit endorsement of policies that continue to degrade San Francisco's Black population (Fracassa 2019)." While the efforts of these leaders did little to halt the removal of Breed from office, it is clear the Rev. Brown's strong stance as a community leader influenced the perspectives of Black voters in the 2018 mayoral election.

In addition to gaining the support of community leaders, Breed gained the endorsement from key Black celebrities and political figures. Former Mayor Willie Brown, the first Black mayor of San Francisco and a once influential figure in Breed's political career, supported her election efforts. As early as the days following Mayor Lee's death, Brown wrote "I hope the Board of Supervisors picks acting Mayor London Breed as interim mayor. I will support her if she chooses to run for mayor in June as well" (Brown 2017). As Brown went on to work as a journalist for the San Francisco Chronicle, he would often write pieces about Breed's campaign and her treatment as mayor. In one such article, Brown wrote, "I've made clear I think she'd be a great mayor" and highlighted the benefit of Breed being ousted from sitting mayor as it garnered her more time for her campaign efforts (Brown 2017). As the first Black mayor of San Francisco, Brown's perspective was both relevant and prominent in the Black community.

Among those who endorsed London Breed also includes former California Senator and 2020 Vice Presidential Candidate Kamala Harris. Harris played an active role in Breed's political development. Breed posted on social media, "I've been proud to call Kamala Harris a friend and mentor" (Breed 2020a). Congresswoman Barbara Lee also endorsed Breed, citing her visionary leadership style and focus on equity: "London has detailed plans for how she will make San Francisco a more just, equitable place for all" (Breed 2018c). The congresswoman would go beyond merely a vocal endorsement of Breed to actively working beside her in political mobilization efforts. Congresswoman Lee collaborated with Breed at her campaign headquarters in Get out the Vote efforts in the days leading up to the 2018 election (Breed 2018c). The Congresswoman's sentiments regarding Breed reflect the symbolic nature of Breed's candidacy and its relevance to the overall narrative of Black female leadership, stating: "Black women can lead and are leading this country into a new day" (Lee 2020).

Breed's positionality as a historic first also landed her the support of esteemed rapper and California native, Snoop Dogg. He tweeted "I'm standing with the women of #ItsOurTimeSF because it's time an accomplished woman led the city" along with a promotional video (Dogg 2018). The video produced by the political action committee It's Our Time San Francisco showed a "rapid fire display of portrait and photos of San Francisco's mayors from 1850 to 2018 …" the text read "168 years. 44 mayors. 1 woman … that was then. This is NOW" (Ioannou 2018). This powerful message made a clear connection between the historic nature of Breed's candidacy as both a woman and a Black person. While the literature notes that Black women are typically the most loyal voters for Black women candidates, Snoop Dogg's endorsement as a highly regarded figure among Black men, with a poignant message about the importance of female leadership, proved that Breed's candidacy could change the trajectory of support in this community (Philpot and Walton 2007).

This endorsement was particularly valuable for Breed's efforts to appeal to younger voters, especially given that election polling data noted Breed as having a stronger support base among older voters. The social media-based endorsement from Snoop Dogg, a well-known voice in the Black California community, was an innovative opportunity for Breed to present herself as a *preferable descriptive representative* to the next generation. According to Suzanne Dovi, voters sift through the field of candidates that they share identities with (also known as descriptive representatives) by increasing the criteria with which they choose a candidate. For a candidate to be considered preferable, Dovi suggests that the candidate must possess "strong mutual relationships with dispossessed subgroups of historically disadvantaged groups" (Dovi 2002). As research conducted by Pew research center shows, this is particularly important for Democrat identifying Millennials and Generation Z-ers, who express strong liberal views on racial equity, gender inclusivity and acceptance of non-binary individuals; many issues that Breed takes a notably moderate stance on (Parker, Graf, and Igielnik 2019).

Breed counters any disconnect between her and younger generations by focusing multiple elements of her campaign on the importance of engaging young Black girls, often visiting, and inviting community schools and university students to attend events with her. She used these speeches as a chance to inspire and empower students with her political history and personal experiences. One student, Jasmin Corley, adeptly summarizes such feelings stating "I love London! She's so inspirational when she talks, it's like the whole room stops" (Knight 2018a). Breed honed in on this in her campaign rhetoric, by discussing her desire to create opportunities for future generations of women to be more engaged in the political process, as voters and future political candidates themselves. In one campaign ad Breed highlights the importance of contemporary decisions in the long-term political process stating, "It's the decisions we make now that will make it possible for the next London Breed" (NA 2018).

Deracializing a Symbolic Moment—Strategies for Garnering the Win

While London Breed's strategy in the Black community prevailed, San Francisco's diverse population and low percentage of Black voters required that she create a much broader, multi-racial coalition to garner the win. In doing so, Breed's campaign became a unique case study on the strengths and limitations of deracialization as a central campaign strategy. Traditionally, political science literature has emphasized deracialization as a pragmatic method for largely male candidates of color to attract white voters and build multi-racial coalitions in majority white jurisdictions (Persons 1993). London Breed breaks this tradition as a female candidate vying for the support of an incredibly diverse population.

As of 2017, San Francisco's population of voting age citizens (CVAP) was approximately 41 percent white, 34 percent Asian, 15 percent Latino, and only 5 percent Black (NA 2017). As a result, Breed's campaign was challenged to develop a policy agenda that appealed to both a white and Asian audience, while maintaining her base of Black voters. Though her campaign was perceived by many Black voters as catering to cultural themes, the following case study will outline how her underlying strategy was largely deracialized. According to McCormick and Jones (1993) successful deracialized campaigns possess three main components: (1) avoidance of public appeals to the Black community, (2) purposeful avoidance of racially divisive issues, and (3) promotion of "non-threatening" images. Using campaign materials, speeches, and social media posts, we examine the elements of Breed's campaign that appear to have been strategically bound by these components.

Avoidance of Public Appeals to the Black Community

As aforementioned, Breed's personal history is one that has explicit ties to the legacy of systemic racism in America. Though her storytelling of her childhood serves as a selling point for many Black voters, Breed often makes the strategic choice to discuss her racialized background in very race neutral terms. Breed often acknowledges the disparate effect that public policy has had on those in the Western Addition, without explicitly naming what the racialized impact was or connecting the issue plaguing that community back to race and racism.

At San Francisco's 2018 March for Our Lives, a national anti-gun violence protest, Breed briefly told the story of losing her close friend to gun violence at only twelve years old. Breed notes that "too often, young people are in neighborhoods and schools impacted by violence because of guns … because lawmakers won't make the hard decisions" (Breed 2018a). In what was an opportunity to use her personal experience to draw the connection between gun violence and poverty in majority minority neighborhoods, Breed chose to maintain a race neutral rhetoric.

Breed's efforts to continuously connect herself and her policy agenda to the story of those in the Western Addition, public housing, and poverty, can be seen as what Christopher Stout calls a positive racial appeal. According to Stout, positive racial appeals occur when a candidate demonstrates their efforts to advance Black policy interests, without attacking outside institutions (Stout 2015). These appeals help connect the candidate to Black voters through a "sense of shared experiences and racial camaraderie" in a way that does not trigger white voters (Stout 2015). Positive racial appeals are integral to a successful campaign because deracialization often does not capture voters of the candidates own race. As witnessed in the case of Harvey Johnson in Jackson, Mississippi, campaigns that lack the nuance to signal loyalty to minority voters without appearing divisive to white voters, will ultimately lose (Orey 2006).

London Breed's campaign was a masterclass in the art of implicit signaling. Breed used her experience as executive director of the African-American Art and Culture Complex (AAACC) as a positive racial appeal. Though the community center was specifically dedicated to "Afrocentric culture, traditions, and values," Breed's discussion of her accomplishments there almost always excludes specific mentions of the benefit to the Black community (NA 2020b). In exchange, Breed often juxtaposes her improvement of the complex as a microcosm of the change she plans to make to the city on behalf of all San Franciscans.

In a profile by the San Francisco Chronicle, journalist Heather Knight asks candidates to take the publication to their favorite place in the city, that sheds light on who they are as a person, not a politician. Breed's profile is done at the AAACC, where she highlights her work to "give the center new energy" by providing physical improvements and increasing resources for the complex's youth. Breed notes "This is exactly what I want San Francisco to be, an amazing place where the bathrooms look great, where the sidewalks look great, where the bus stops look great, where you don't see glass all over the streets" (Knight 2018).

Breed's choice to be profiled at the AAACC is an implicit appeal and show of authenticity to Black voters who've found a home and community in the complex. However, her focus on the material improvement of the complex is an explicit appeal to conservative leaning voters who take issue with the unkemptness of San Francisco streets, often because of a large population of homeless individuals (a point Breed often makes in her discussions on homelessness). Obviously omitted from Breed's discussion is a commentary on the conditions that created the need for such improvements, and the policies that may have sustained the complex's underdevelopment prior to her leadership there. Ultimately, Breed's discussion of any racially pointed subject always tilts back to her racially transcendent policy agenda, homelessness, housing equity, and public safety.

Avoidance of Racially Divisive Issues

One can infer that London Breed's avoidance of racially divisive issues ultimately shaped her campaign policy agenda. The issues she centers on, homelessness, housing equity, and public safety, each address pressing and historical issues for San Francisco, while carrying no explicit racial leaning. Breed's skillful framing allows her to discuss issues that border racial divisiveness without alienating conservative white and/or Asian voters. When asked about the importance of San Francisco being a sanctuary city, Breed opts for inclusive framing, discussing the immigrant community as one that is important to San Francisco, and noting that immigration policies impact "all of us in our city" (Breed 2018b). Breed argues: "how fair is it to take a 20-year-old kid … and deport them to a country they are not even familiar with" (Breed 2018b). Even in her examples, she takes a neutral route by excluding the races, nationalities, or countries of origin of the San Francisco immigrant population. Breed's framing allows this policy stance to appear beneficial to both the immigrant community, and those who don't perceive themselves as directly impacted by immigration policy.

Data from Survey USA further exemplifies how voters responded to such appeals. This survey includes several items measuring issue importance comparatively, measuring the prioritization of housing, the economy, crime, homelessness, education, gentrification, and transportation concerns. Respondents were asked which issue was most important in San Francisco. We will use this ranking to analyze which issues drive support for the candidates, particularly Breed. If Breed supporters demonstrate high regard for race neutral issues such as the economy, it would indicate an effective implementation of a deracialized agenda in the Breed campaign. Table 6.2 supports this inference, indicating housing was the most important issue to Breed supporters, with 36 percent of voters noting it as the priority, followed by the related issue of homelessness at 29 percent.

Promotion of Nonthreatening Images

According to Wright and Middleton (2004), promoting non-threatening images requires a candidate to abstain from responses that would cause them to appear confrontational and avoid personal associations that would racialize their campaign. As the campaign ad in Figure 6.1 showcases, Breed took explicit efforts

TABLE 6.2 Most Important Issue by Candidate Supporters

%	Leno Supporters	Kim Supporters	Breed Supporters
Housing Prices	41	25	36
Economy & Jobs	5	14	3
Crime	9	10	13
Homelessness	25	25	29
Public Transportation	1	5	1
Traffic & Congestion	11	9	8
Quality of Education	5	7	6
City Gentrification	3	6	2
Other	0	0	2

Source: Survey USA 2018 San Francisco Election Polling.

FIGURE 6.1 London Breed Campaign Banner

Photo Credit: 2018 London Breed for San Francisco Mayor Campaign

to assure voters that she was concerned for the wellbeing of *all* San Francisco residents, rather than appealing solely to minoritized communities.

Breed also accomplishes a non-threatening image by consistently imagining her campaign through the eyes of the youth. She began this by intentionally displaying photos and footage of her interactions with children in each of her campaign videos. Breed's evocation of the campaign's significance to youth is often a strategy to disarm and deflect interviewers who probe on the racial significance of her campaign. When asked how she feels about being the first Black female mayor, Breed redirects her answer to focus on young girls, noting, "What's great about it is getting to see so many young girls wanting to be Mayor" (Herrera 2018).

Breed's reframing toward the youth is a consistent trend that allows her to inspire Black voters while also staying race neutral when discussing potentially divisive topics. In a May tweet, Breed addresses the "mud-slinging and personal attacks" that she's received. She does so by emphasizing the relevance of this campaign to the youth, stating that "SF has given so much to me. Let's make sure the next generation has the same opportunity." This statement is accompanied by a video montage of multiracial youthful faces, ending with a group of children who emphatically yell "London!" (Breed 2018c).

In her signature style, Breed seals the deal on her commitment to the youth and to her community by officially accepting her victory at Rosa Parks Elementary school in the Western Addition (Sabatini 2018). Breed's victory speech addresses her bold plans to build housing, increase mental health services, and to connect San Franciscans with drug addictions to treatment services. On the heels of a historic election for the Black community, Breed maintains her focus on the SF community as whole, reminding all voters of the benefit she aims to bring.

Deracialization in the Context of Competition

As we consider the organization of Breed's campaign, and the elements contributing to her success, it is crucial to consider the electoral context she operated in. San Francisco operates elections using a ranked choice voting system which eliminates the need for run-off elections. In this system, voters rank all candidates in order of preference, with a maximum number of 10 candidates on the ballot. A candidate wins if they receive a majority of first choice votes. If no one wins a majority, then the least voted for candidate is eliminated and their voters' second choice is counted. This cycle continues until a candidate becomes the majority winner through a combination of first and second choice votes (Kambhampaty 2019).

Eight candidates made the ballot for the 2018 mayoral election in San Francisco. The top three candidates were London Breed, Jane Kim, and Mark Leno. All three of whom would have been historic firsts for the San Francisco mayor's office; Breed as the first Black woman, Kim as the first Asian woman, and Leno as the first openly gay mayor of the city. Because of this ranked choice ballot, candidates are incentivized to form alliances with one another to garner second choice votes. To undermine Breed as the race's front runner, Kim and Leno agreed to encourage their supporters to list one another as their second-choice candidate (Berman 2018). Despite this coalition of candidates whose descriptive characteristics match most San Francisco's population, Breed prevailed.

Leno's supporters were white voters in the Baby Boomer generation. Table 6.3 displays the demographic breakdown of the candidates' supporters. As a white man running for office, Leno did not have to contend with concerns regarding the focus of race in his campaign, unlike Breed and Kim who were expected to address issues from their perspective as women of color.

Board of Supervisors member Jane Kim's supporters included residents who were most concerned with crime and city gentrification, two heavily racialized issues. Kim successfully appealed to Asian community leaders garnering endorsements from leaders of local Asian organizations such as the API Commissioners and the Founder of the Chinatown Community Development Center. However, Kim failed to garner support from the women base, trailing behind Breed and Leno as female voters' third choice candidate for mayor.

Breed's deracialized campaign is incredibly important when considering the political ideology of her supporters. We find that most Breed's supporters were moderates followed by conservatives rather than liberals. At this point, one should remember San Francisco is a predominantly Democrat city with only 11 percent of SurveyUSA respondents identifying as Republican. Therefore, these may not be conservatives and moderates in the traditional ideological sense of the words. Historically, Black Americans are more likely to demonstrate conservative ideologies rather than identify as liberal (Tate 1993). Even considering this, Black Americans make up 5 percent of the voting population in San Francisco, and most supporters are moderate. Therefore, there must be another explanation for this ideological split in support. This moderate base of support could serve as indication that Breed's deracialized campaign was successfully allowing her to transition her appeal beyond her social identity.

TABLE 6.3 2018 Mayoral Candidates Support by Demographics

	Richie Greenberg	Mark Leno	Amy Weiss	Angelo Alioto	Jane Kim	Ellen Lee Zhou	Michelle Bravo	London Breed
Sex (%)								
Male	5	29	2	7	15	2	2	15
Female	4	14	1	11	12	1	1	25
Age (%)								
18–34	10	17	2	4	28	2	0	11
35–49	3	12	3	6	15	3	4	21
50–64	3	35	1	11	6	0	1	21
65+	1	26	1	14	6	2	1	25
Race (%)								
White	4	27	1	10	14	1	1	17
Black	0	3	11	12	1	2	9	48
Hispanic	9	19	0	6	9	0	2	23
Asian	5	18	1	7	18	4	1	16
Party ID (%)								
Republican	15	16	0	18	9	3	6	10
Democrat	4	24	2	9	14	1	2	24
Independ	1	21	1	5	14	1	0	11
Ideology (%)								
Conservative	8	11	0	6	16	3	5	21
Moderate	4	22	2	12	14	1	0	23
Liberal	4	28	2	5	13	1	2	16
Income (%)								
<40K	3	16	4	11	13	0	0	21
$40K	3	33	0	10	12	1	1	23
>80K	5	20	2	7	15	2	2	18

Source: Survey USA 2018 Election Poll: Sample size (n): 800 San Francisco adults.

Breed's social transcendency came with both its benefits and challenges, however. As her prominence grew in the white and Asian communities, Black voters took notice of a lack of effort put into campaigning in Black neighborhoods. Many voters took issue with her absence at Black community events, especially events geared toward the improvement of the Western Addition (Lapidus 2018). Her major competitors, Jane Kim and Mark Leno made themselves present to advocate for Western Addition housing in jeopardy of being demolished, while voters said Breed was not available (Lapidus 2018).

Celebration Despite Skepticism

Though some Black voters remained skeptical of Breed's commitment to the Black community, her win was seen as a triumph for the entire San Franciscan population. Black voters celebrated with hope for what she could become as a leader, what the community would become under her leadership, and what the nation could learn from San Francisco's new trajectory toward racial equality (Altizer 2018). John William Templeton, historian of Black culture and business in San Francisco notes:

> [Breed's election] reflects the best of San Francisco as a western sanctuary where people who didn't have opportunities in other places could come.
>
> *Fuller 2018*

This hope and optimism were best put on display at the city's Interfaith celebration of Breed's victory. An amalgamation of religious organizations and community organizations came out in support of Breed, as the Reverend Dr. Frederick Douglas Haynes, III, Pastor of Friendship West Baptist Church in Dallas, Texas delivered a fiery message to congregants on the importance of Breed's election. Haynes, likened Breed to the Biblical figure Esther, who is known for her role in stopping the impending extermination of the Jewish population (Gillette 2018). Like Esther, Breed was regarded by her community as a chosen leader, with the weighty responsibility of redeeming her people.

Politics and Protests: Breed's Governing Style

At the onset of Breed's term as the first Black woman Mayor of San Francisco, she focused her efforts on addressing the homelessness and housing affordability crisis. Breed dedicated over 300 million dollars in an affordable housing bond to building more housing options in the city. She would go on to reallocate 5.8 million in the city's budget to provide legal representation for tenants facing eviction, earning San Francisco the credit of being California's first city to offer full defense to tenants (Breed 2019). These are a few examples of her fiscal and legislative efforts to create more affordable housing options. The disparity in housing access would soon become exaggerated by the Coronavirus pandemic.

Breed successfully navigated a deracialized campaign in the 2018 special election and through her re-election campaign in 2019. However, this strategy was no longer feasible given the global Black Lives Matter (BLM) protests in 2020 addressing police brutality and systemic racial inequity. As policing largely falls under the authority of local political leadership, many initiatives such as the "8 Can't Wait" project, have turned toward local politicians in their demands for police reforms (NA 2020a). Police forces fall under the jurisdictions of city and state governments making it imperative to consider Breed's response to these protests. Thus, the question emerges: how might a Black Mayor who ran a deracialized campaign respond to an eruption of protests seeking racial equity in her city?

While Breed as a Black woman with political power may be expected to respond directly to these protests, the deracialized nature of Breed's campaign draws this expectation into question. First, we consider the environment Breed responded within during the protests. San Francisco fulfills the use of force policy suggestions from campaigns such as the "8 Can't Wait" project. These policies can in part be attributed to recommendations after the federal investigation of the San Francisco police officer's shooting of Mario Woods in 2015 (Fracassa & Cassidy, 2020). City officials failed to implement all the recommendations, but some of the reform measures were implemented prior to the 2018 election.

These reforms established a foundation for Breed to address protest demands in a somewhat deracialized manner, framing her response as a continuation of previous work. However, Breed instead chose to center her response to these protests in her racial identity, attending a demonstration and reminding her constituents of the killing of her cousin by a police officer prior to her political career. These actions were a clear divergence from her traditional strategies.

Breed's shift in rhetoric came at an opportune time, in which the risk associated with racialized rhetoric was lower. During these protests, public opinion for the BLM movement positively shifted with most Americans of varying races increasing in support for BLM (Parker, Horowitz, & Anderson 2020). Breed took the opportunity presented by the BLM protests to reorient her strategy and center her identity and experience in policy agenda.

Among Breed's plans for police reform include the demilitarization of police, alternative responses to non-criminal activity, addressing police bias, and budget reallocation (Breed 2020b). Alternative police response includes replacing officers with social workers and counselors for non-criminal emergency services calls. Breed initiated protocols for law enforcement hiring policies including screening for racial bias and expanding on the SFPD's implicit bias training program. Another component of her reforms includes budget reallocation, directing law enforcement funds toward investing in marginalized communities particularly the city's Black community.

Conclusion

Our analysis of the 2018 San Francisco Mayoral race aimed to uncover how the theories of descriptive representation, symbolic empowerment and deracialization worked together to explain the election of the first Black female mayor in a diverse, yet predominantly white major city. London Breed's 2018 run for Mayor was an archetype of a successfully implemented deracialized political campaign that effectively captured the hearts and minds of the Black community. Breed's campaign was up against two descriptive representatives, who more closely matched the identities of much of the San Francisco population. Despite the presence and impact of coalitions that targeted her campaign's demise, Breed successfully marketed herself as a moderate Democrat with a broad policy focus and an inherent connection to the struggles of the suffering Black community.

Our case study on her media coverage, social media posts and campaign materials exemplified how she employed messaging of her personal history to target Black voters, while modeling McCormick and Jones' tenets of deracialization. Breed's focus on race neutral policies such as health care, housing, and homelessness allowed her to cast a wide net for voters of all races. Her strategic avoidance of stigmatizing issues, topics, and associations helped her to maintain non-Black voters, while her implicit positive appeals to her Black identity helped energize and win over a majority of Black San Franciscans. Breed strategically downplayed the role of race in her upbringing, telling her own story in a way that appealed to even non-Black voters by focusing on the relevance of her campaign to the youth.

Out of necessity and urgency, Breed's political style evolved from running on a deracialized campaign to centering her intersectional identity in her governing and response to community crisis' such as the BLM protests and the coronavirus pandemic. As many elected officials who run on a deracialized campaign must do, Breed is now developing how to best chart a course from a race neutral appeal to a race centric application of public policy. Breed's reelection campaign materials indicate that she will continue shifting her approach, as community preferences realign to supporting racial equity in politics.

Note

1 We use the topline report of these data for this draft and have requested, but have not received, the raw data from the survey investigators for our future analysis.

References

Altizer, Drew. 2018. "Historic Inauguration of London Breed Brings Plenty to City Hall." *The Nob Hill Gazette*. https://nobhillgazette.com/london-breeds-big-day/ (September 6, 2020).

Berman, Russell. 2018. "Rival Candidates Try an Unusual Election Message: Vote for Both of Us." *The Atlantic*. www.theatlantic.com/politics/archive/2018/05/san-francisco-mayor-jane-kim-mark-leno-ranked-choice-voting/561053/ (June 28, 2020).

Boney, Jeffrey. 2018. "London Breed Overcomes Adversity to Become SF's First Black Female Mayor." *Sacramento Observer*. https://sacobserver.com/2018/07/london-breed-overcomes-adversity-to-become-san-franciscos-first-black-female-mayor/ (September 6, 2020).

Breed, London. 2018a. "I'm Inspired by All of the Young Leaders..." www.instagram.com/londonbreed/ (July 8, 2020).

Breed, London. 2018b. "London Breed Interview." *KTVU*. www.youtube.com/watch?v=BiE-CZLbhAE (May 27, 2020).

Breed, London. 2018c. "Our Diversity Is Our Biggest Strength...." *Twitter*. https://twitter.com/LondonBreed/status/996504234072817664 (July 7, 2020).

Breed, London. 2019. "London Breed on Housing." *Re-Elect Mayor London Breed*. https://twitter.com/LondonBreed/status/1003784785590751232 (September 15, 2020).

Breed, London. 2020a. "Breed on Twitter." *Twitter*.

https://twitter.com/LondonBreed/status/1293281460141477889 (September 15, 2020).

Breed, London. 2020b. *Twitter.* https://twitter.com/LondonBreed/status/100378478559 0751232 (September 15, 2020).

Brown, Willie. 2017. "'Caretaker' Mayor for S.F.? It's a Terrible Idea.'" *San Francisco Chronicle,* December 23.

Chappel, Bill, and Richard Gonzales. 2017. "San Francisco Mayor Ed Lee Dies at Age 65." *NPR.org.* www.npr.org/sections/thetwo-way/2017/12/12/570104228/san-francisco-mayor-edwin-lee-dies-at-age-65 (July 8, 2020).

Dogg, Snoop. 2018. "Snoop Dogg on Twitter." *Twitter.* https://twitter.com/SnoopDogg/sta tus/971834188461568000 (September 15, 2020).

Dovi, Suzanne. 2002. "Preferable Descriptive Representatives: Will Just Any Woman, Black, or Latino Do?" *American Political Science Review* 96(4): 729–743.

Downs, Anthony. 1957. *An Economic Theory of Democracy.* New York: Harper.

Fracassa, Dominic. 2019. "Black Leaders Slam 'Racist' Breed Critics." *San Francisco Chronicle,* October 14, 2019.

Fracassa, Dominic, and Megan Cassidy. 2020. "SF Mayor Releases Police Reform Plan to Deal with Racism, Use of Force, Homelessness, Mental Health," *San Francisco Chronicle,* June 11, 2020. www.sfchronicle.com/crime/article/Defund-San-Francisco-police-Chief-Bill-Scott-15328129.php.

Fuller, Thomas. 2016. "The Loneliness of Being Black in San Francisco." *The New York Times,* July 21, 2016. www.nytimes.com/2016/07/21/us/black-exodus-from-san-francisco.html (September 6, 2020).

Fuller, Thomas. 2018. "California Today: History in San Francisco With the Election of a Black Female Mayor." *The New York Times,* June 14, 2018. www.nytimes.com/2018/06/14/us/california-today-london-breed-san-francisco.html (September 6, 2020).

Garofoli, Joe. 2018. "London Breed Is the Exception—Why Few Blacks Rise to Power in Bay Area." *San Francisco Chronicle,* July 18, 2018. www.sfchronicle.com/politics/article/London-Breed-is-the-exception-why-few-blacks-13086677.php (September 6, 2020).

Gillette, Frankie. 2018. "Faith Community Joins in Prayer for Mayor London Breed." *Oakland Post,* July 13, 2018. www.postnewsgroup.com/52794/ (September 6, 2020).

Hernandez, Pedro. 2018. "Data and Maps from the 2018 San Francisco Mayoral Election." *Fair Vote California.* www.fairvoteca.org/data_and_maps_from_the_2018_san_francisco_mayoral_election.

Herrera, Julianne. 2018. "London Breed: 'I Will Defend This City with All My Might.'" *KRON4,* June 15, 2018. www.kron4.com/news/bay-area/london-breed-i-will-defend-this-city-with-all-my-might/ (July 8, 2020).

Ioannou, Filipa. 2018. "Snoop Dogg Endorses London Breed for Mayor." *San Francisco Gate,* March 9, 2018. www.sfgate.com/politics/article/Snoop-Dogg-sf-mayor-London-Breed-celebrity-endorse-12741625.php?utm_source=dlvr.it&utm_medium=twitter.

Jones, Allen. 2018. "White Privilege Ousts Black Mayor." *San Francisco Bay View,* January 28, 2018. https://sfbayview.com/2018/01/white-privilege-ousts-black-mayor/ (September 15, 2020).

Kambhampaty, Anna. 2019. "What is Ranked Choice Voting? Here's How it Works." *Time,* November 6, 2019. https://time.com/5718941/ranked-choice-voting/.

Knight, Heather. 2018a. "Breed Overcame Odds, Says City Can as Well." *San Francisco Chronicle,* July 5, 2018.

Knight, Heather. 2018b. "London Breed Cites Her Experience as Path to Transforming San Francisco." *San Francisco Chronicle,* April 6, 2018. www.sfchronicle.com/news/article/London-Breed-cites-experience-transforming-SF-12806970.php (May 27, 2020).

KTVU. 2018. "London Breed's Western Addition Success Story." *KTVU,* June 14, 2018. www.ktvu.com/news/london-breeds-western-addition-success-story.

Lapidus, Sarah. 2018. "African-American Community Hopes Mayor Breed Will Step Up." *Bay News Rising,* September 28, 2018. https://baynewsrising.org/2018/09/28/african-american-community-hopes-mayor-breed-will-step-up-2/ (September 6, 2020).

Lee, Barbara. 2020. *Congresswoman Barbara Lee Supports London Breed for Mayor.* www.youtube.com/watch?v=5U6SY0JV5Oo&ab_channel=LondonBreedforMayor (September 15, 2020).

Levy-Wolins, Aaron. 2018. "Farrell Named Interim SF Mayor at Contentious Board Meeting." *El Tecolote,* January 25, 2018. http://eltecolote.org/content/en/news/farrell-named-interim-sf-mayor-at-contentious-board-meeting/ (September 6, 2020).

McCormick, Joseph, and Charles E. Jones. 1993. "The Conceptualization of Deracialization: Thinking Through the Dilemma." In *Dilemmas of Black Politics: Issues of Leadership and Strategy,* edited by Georgia Persons, 66–84. New York: Harper Collins.

McCubbin, Hamilton I., Elizabeth A. Thompson, Anne I. Thompson, and Jo A. Futrell, eds. 1998. *Resiliency in African-American Families.* Thousand Oaks, CA: Sage.

NA. 2017. "2017 CVAP—San Francisco." *Social Explorer.* www.socialexplorer.com/tables/CVAP_2017_5yr (July 5, 2020).

NA. 2018. *The Next London Breed.* www.youtube.com/watch?v=y5Z11G1kpJE&ab_channel=LondonBreedforMayor (September 15, 2020).

NA. 2020a. "8 Can't Wait." https://8cantwait.org/ (September 15, 2020).

NA. 2020b. "About." *African American Art and Culture Complex.* http://aaacc.org/about/ (July 8, 2020).

Orey, Byron D'Andra. 2006. "Deracialization or Racialization: The Making of a Black Mayor in Jackson, Mississippi." *Politics & Policy* 34(4): 814–836.

Parker, Kim, Juliana Horowitz, and Anderson, Monica. 2020. "Amid Protests, Majorities Across Racial and Ethnic Groups Express Support for the Black Lives Matter Movement." Washington, D.C. Pew Research Center.

Parker, Kim, Nikki Graf, and Ruth Igielnik. 2019. "Generation Z Looks a Lot Like Millennials on Key Social and Political Issues." *Pew Research Center's Social & Demographic Trends Project.* www.pewsocialtrends.org/2019/01/17/generation-z-looks-a-lot-like-millennials-on-key-social-and-political-issues/ (September 14, 2020).

Pepin, Elizabeth, and Lewis Watts. 2006. *Harlem of the West: The San Francisco Fillmore Jazz Era.* San Francisco, CA: Chronicle Books.

Perry, Huey L. 1991. "Deracialization as an Analytical Construct in American Urban Politics." *Urban Affairs Quarterly* 27(2): 181–191.

Persons, Georgia Anne. 1993. *Dilemmas of Black Politics: Issues of Leadership and Strategy.* New York: HarperCollins.

Philpot, Tasha S., and Hanes Walton. 2007. "One of Our Own: Black Female Candidates and the Voters Who Support Them." *American Journal of Political Science* 51(1): 49–62.

Associated Press (AP). 2018. "Pick for Interim San Francisco Mayor Upsets Black Activists." *Access WDUN.* https://accesswdun.com/print/2018/1/629207 (September 6, 2020).

Robertson, Lin. 2018. "London Breed, You Are My Mayor Too." *San Francisco Bay View,* July 14, 2018. https://sfbayview.com/2018/07/london-breed-you-are-my-mayor-too/ (September 15, 2020).

Sabatini, Joshua. 2018. "Mayor-Elect Breed Visits Her Old School, Vows to 'Change What Is Normal." *The San Francisco Examiner,* June 14, 2018. www.sfexaminer.com/news/mayor-elect-breed-visits-her-old-school-vows-to-change-what-is-normal/ (July 8, 2020).

Schneider, Benjamin, and Alastair Boone. 2018. "What Just Happened in San Francisco?" *Bloomberg.com.* www.bloomberg.com/news/articles/2018-01-25/explaining-the-tense-mayoral-shakeup-in-san-francisco (September 9, 2020).

Shafer, Scott. "Political Uproar as Mark Farrell Replaces London Breed as S.F. Mayor." *KQED,* January 23, 2018. www.kqed.org/news/11643930/political-outrage-as-mark-farrell-replaces-london-breed-as-s-f-s-acting-mayor (July 8, 2020).

Stout, Christopher T. 2015. *Bringing Race Back in: Black Politicians, Deracialization, and Voting Behavior in the Age of Obama.* Charlottesville, VA: University of Virginia Press.

Tate, Katherine. 1993. *From Protest to Politics: The New Black Voters in American Elections.* Cambridge, MA: Harvard University Press.

Thompson, Walter. 2016. "How Urban Renewal Destroyed the Fillmore in Order to Save It – Smart Growth Online." https://smartgrowth.org/how-urban-renewal-destroyed-the-fillmore-in-order-to-save-it/ (September 9, 2020).

U.S. Census Bureau (2018). San Francisco, 2013-2018 American Community Survey 5-year estimates. Retrieved from https://www.socialexplorer.com/tables/ACS2018_5yr

Wright, Sharon D., and Richard T. Middleton. 2004. "The Limitations of the Deracialization Concept in the 2001 Los Angeles Mayoral Election." *Political Research Quarterly* 52(2): 283–293.

7

HISTORIC FIRSTS IN U.S. ELECTIONS

A Conclusion

Evelyn M. Simien

By all counts, voter turnout soared during the 2018 Congressional midterm and the 2020 American presidential elections. Historic firsts have since received an unprecedented amount of media attention for their legislative advocacy and progressive policy positions. As trailblazers, they change the nature of political representation as we know it and expose the complex intersections of inequality and marginalization at work via the conservative backlash and voter suppression efforts we witness in the aftermath of their elections. The historic candidacies of the gubernatorial, congressional, and mayoral candidates featured here—Andrew Gillum, Ilhan Omar, Ayanna Pressley, Rashida Tlaib, and London Breed—challenge the electoral norms and confront the political institutions that have long advantaged white men. As evidenced by the line-up of candidates from 2018, and the record number of women and men of color who ran for the American presidency in 2020, the gains made for historic firsts were concentrated among Democrats at every level of office and have practical implications for the substantive representation of minority interests writ large.

While evaluating their respective game-changing performances offers keen insights into the future of American elections, researching "firsts" for women and men of color across levels of office serves as a reminder of the work left to be done to ensure that our political institutions reflect the full range of constituencies they serve. As suggested earlier, the election of historic firsts has palpable effects on American voters and the practice of democracy especially when such candidates disrupt the (white male) status quo in American politics and challenge basic assumptions of how, where, and which candidates can achieve electoral success. Take, for example, U.S. Representatives Omar and Pressley, who embraced their race-gender identities as electoral assets and not as hurdles to overcome. They drew upon their distinct lived experiences and challenged the valuation and

DOI: 10.4324/9781003213925-7

expression of stereotypically masculine credentials for officeholding with identity-based and values-laden appeals. Nonetheless, there is very little evidence to suggest that the significance of such trailblazing candidates is acknowledged by the discipline of political science generally and the American politics subfield specifically. In fact, the silence is astounding.

Having elevated the status of historic firsts as subjects of scholarly importance, I offer some brief reflections on the possible implications of their breakthrough elections for scholars in political science and practitioners on the campaign field—for example, the progressives among them in the U.S. Congress have taken moderate Democrats and the federal government to task on infrastructure and reconciliation bills with their prioritization of climate change and social spending being brought to the fore during the height of negotiations. Along the way, I discuss how the symbolic empowerment framework might be applied to new cases. The goal is: to provide a baseline against which other historic firsts might "fit" categorically to achieve broader knowledge through the analysis of a wider range of cases based on a set of commonalties deemed important for comparison. While probing the generality of past findings and recognizing the difficulties of establishing equivalence among contexts, the symbolic empowerment framework helps researchers establish sufficiently similar patterns for which to evaluate them. The expectation is that future researchers will pick up where I and others have left off with this collection of original essays.

Take, for example, the 2021 Georgia U.S. Senate run-off elections with historic first candidates Raphael Warnock and Jon Ossoff. The broader context remains marked by the Trump era; however, future research must consider a larger set of cases that vary by gender, race, ethnicity, and time simultaneously, so commonalities and differences might be systematically coded and problematized, but without distorting the overarching framework. Relatedly, I propose theoretical and methodological ways of advancing the study of historic first candidates using a relational approach to analyze them—for example, I would argue that the symbolic empowerment framework should be extended to include new historic firsts from before, during, and after the Trump era.

Notably, there is no comparable collection of original essays about historic first candidates. Instead of investigating what conditions are ripe for historic firsts, I ask: Do trailblazing candidates bring formally politically inactive people into the electoral process? This is the key question that motivates this study of *Historic Firsts in U.S. Elections*. Using a case study approach, contributors to this edited volume leverage poll data, voter turnout reports, news coverage, stump speeches, campaign materials, as well as interviews with candidates and constituents alike to determine how and to what extent historic firsts unite diverse electorates, establish multiracial coalitions, and invoke a strong affective emotion like pride among those they come to represent once elected to office. Contributors to this collection revisit and reevaluate breakthrough contests, including the behaviors of *both* the candidates *and* voters. By systematically comparing the tools and artifacts of each campaign, they elucidate and showcase the ways in which historic first candidates change the face of American politics. The consistent refrain in the analyses of each game-changing performance underscores the need to look beyond women, racial and ethnic minorities, as well as young people as monolithic groups to understand the influence of historic first candidates on diverse electorates especially among newly registered and first-time voters. The nuances of these campaigns, or rather the content of their political messages, are often tied the candidate's race-gender identity as well as their targeted approach to campaigning.

While historic first candidates focus most intently and extensively on signaling an expressed commitment to certain populations and stress the importance of their policy interests, they also signal by virtue of their presence the progress that numerically underrepresented groups have made in electoral politics on the state, local, and national level. To reiterate, the moment when historic first candidates enter the electoral arena and the campaign ensues is described in terms of contextual effects that are symbolically empowering. The cumulative effect of their multiple identities and the historic nature of their campaigns stoke the desire to vote and participate in other ways, which compels us to think about their lasting impact as they influence nonvoting behavior as well.

Researching American campaigns and elections in this way remains relatively under-explored in political science, given the explicit focus on historic first candidates. The present approach constitutes but one way of applying the symbolic empowerment framework to several cases at once. Why does this matter? The answer is that it matters because based on the evidenced shown here, it is not simply group identity but the ability to exhibit an awareness of inequalities along multiple dimensions that inform connections across privilege as well as subordination that results in viable electoral success for historic first candidates in some of the most racially and ethnically diverse urban milieus.

This intellectual project traces multiple aspects of historic first campaigns, starting with personal biographies of each preferable descriptive representative and the grassroots activities that afford them the opportunities to emerge as viable candidates. Historic first candidates are different because they understand the needs of multiply disadvantaged groups in ways that other more traditional candidates do not, and because many, if not most of them, demonstrate a praxis orientation. It must be noted that disciplinary conventions in political science import a range of assumptions and truth claims about what constitutes success and contributes to the erasure of historic first candidates who fail to win election, dismissing them as quixote figures and their campaigns as inconsequential despite their use of the electoral system differently. Contributors consistently detail the electoral fortunes of historic first candidates, assuming they are constrained by political opportunity structures differently than incumbents especially, and their opponents in co-ethnic communities. This edited volume situates the main subject—that being, in this case: a historic first candidate—strategically in terms of identity, geography, and temporality.

As I have argued elsewhere (Simien 2015), historic first candidates must be judged on their own terms rather than those used to evaluate more traditional candidates. Strict vote counts or turnout do not fully capture their long-term impact, which exceeds the timeline of any single election. Trailblazers like Andrew Gillum pave the way and create the opportunity for future candidates and subsequent victories especially when their unexpected game-changing performances set them apart. The impact factor of such historic first candidates cannot be assessed by traditional measures, given their alternative performance goals include non-voting participation and affords others a "coat-tails" advantage. It is reasonable to assume that historic firsts pay the "dues" and improve the electoral prospects for future candidates to be taken seriously. As Sharon Wright Austin rightly observes, Gillum lost to his Republican opponent Ron DeSantis by a razor thin margin and became one of the few African-Americans to emerge as a serious contender for a statewide executive office. Thus, it would be useful to distinguish between winners and losers for the purpose of identifying a pioneer cohort. To introduce a range of empirical cases into the framework and not abandon broad comparisons would increase the reach of the symbolic empowerment framework and add to a general discussion of historic first candidates.

As shown in the chapters that precede this conclusion, congresswomen of color like Ilhan Omar, Rashida Tlaib, and Ayanna Pressley are uniquely attentive to the needs and interests of those who, like them, are multiply disadvantaged. Such barrier-breaking figures matter insofar as they emerge onto the political scene as advocates who champion more liberal and progressive policies generally, but especially for the greater attention paid to and substantive representation of disadvantaged subgroups within marginalized communities. These women of color political elites possess substantial political qualifications, including long careers of public service. Contributors Stefanie Chambers and Laurel Elder demonstrate the usefulness of intersectionality as an analytic tool for studying the complexities of race, gender, and political representation with rigor and sophistication when studying U.S. Representative Omar of the 5th Congressional District in Minnesota. While attending to the behavior and impact of women of color elected officials like Omar is important, other contributors like Michael Minta, offer new insights into the distinctive, yet varying, contributions women of color like U.S. Representative Tlaib of Michigan's 13th District make to policy agendas once serving in office. Still, contributors like Lauren Jones and myself draw critical attention to the particularities of Black women like Ayanna Pressley whose formidable campaign revealed the challenges faced by high quality challengers opposing long-term incumbents who represent the default identity category in electoral politics—a white male—and when voters could not rely on partisanship as a cue.

As political scientists, who possess our own views about the merits of these candidates and their historic elections, we have addressed the how and why questions regarding their performance. How does race and gender affect who gets elected, as well as who is voting? What does the historic first candidate's ground game reveal? Why do diverse electorates make a difference? While this project will *not* put to rest the debate set forth by skeptics about the usefulness of identity-based appeals and values-driven rhetoric to advance a campaign, it will most certainly inform our thinking about long-standing questions on the impact of more race neutral, deracialized electioneering techniques void of such an emphasis in comparable electoral environments. The timeless debate is reignited by historic first candidates Rashida Tlaib and London Breed, as they set new precedents and have us reconsider everything, we think we know about how change occurs in local and national elections with diverse electorates.

In conclusion, the case studies play an important role in knowledge production. The sort of specific, intensive, and detailed data presented here is required in advance of considering what are the right methods for forecasting results across similar subjects and comparable target populations. Until more data is collected for formal modeling or large-N analysis, the case studies serve to spotlight features of an electoral system and the contests within it. The rationale behind said approach is to amass qualitative data and evidence for future use. If one is seeking to understand what variables are relevant on the ground and in particular contexts, the crucial information these case studies provide will bear on the applicability of causal generalizations to be empirically tested through statistical and quantitative means in future studies.

Reference

Simien, Evelyn M. 2015. *Historic Firsts: How Symbolic Empowerment Changes U.S. Politics.* New York: Oxford University Press.

INDEX

Note: Page numbers in **bold** indicate tables; those in *italics* indicate figures.